Be Your Own Broker

Be Your Own Broker

Using the Internet to Discover Emerging Growth Stocks

Paul H. Christiansen

Writer's Showcase presented by *Writer's Digest*
San Jose New York Lincoln Shanghai

Be Your Own Broker
Using the Internet to Discover Emerging Growth Stocks

Published by Writer's Showcase presented by *Writer's Digest*
an imprint of iUniverse.com, Inc.

For information address:
iUniverse.com, Inc.
620 North 48th Street
Suite 201
Lincoln, NE 68504-3467
www.iuniverse.com

ISBN: 0-595-09798-7

Printed in the United States of America

Dedicated with love to my daughters Randi and Paula, and to my son Guy.

Table of Contents

Introduction   *vii*

Chapter 1...The times they are a'changing   *1*
> The Internet and the online brokerage industry are shaking
> the foundations of the investment industry. These changes
> are also presenting challenges to individual investors, who
> will have to learn how to adapt to the new order.

Chapter 2...Why the changes were inevitable   *19*
> A review of past inefficiencies and conflicts of interest reveals
> why changes were probably inevitable.

Chapter 3...Doing your own research   *37*
> Specific, proven tools are identified–along with guides on
> how to use them–to help individual investors discover.
> emerging growth stocks.

Chapter 4...Opportunities for all investors   *71*
> Even individuals with modest investment funds can fully
> participate in the methods outlined in this book.

Chapter 5...The necessary financial controls   *89*
> Three spreadsheets that will help you to measure your invest-
> ment performance, along with detailed instructions on how
> to use them.

Chapter 6…Some Lessons Learned   119

Appendix   139
A collection of articles about the Information Technology industry.

Introduction

Being a stockbroker should be one of the most gratifying and rewarding occupations available to anyone. The potential for gratification comes from successfully helping clients increase their wealth by consistently matching or beating the performance of the popular market averages. During the decade of the 1990s that level of performance would have put a smile on the face of any investor. What's the potential reward for a broker who helps clients to achieve that level of performance? A veteran broker with more than five years in the business could have the potential for an annual income ranging from mid-six digits to low seven digits; in other words, anywhere from $500,000 per year to over $1 million per year.

Helping clients to match or beat the performance of any of the popular market averages should be a breeze for an experienced stockbroker, especially those that have the support of research departments that scan the universe of stocks looking for potential winners. After all, Wall Street research departments have been the fountains of information from which most investors drink. Until recently, very few sources of investment information have been able to rival the ability of Wall Street research to identify industry segments and specific companies that are generating above-average revenue and earnings growth. But is it a breeze? How difficult is it for any stockbroker to consistently match or beat the performance of the popular market averages? Let me try to answer that question with a several questions.

Do you think that brokers would have to pester folks with unsolicited telephone calls if their brokerage firms had a certifiable reputation for providing advice that enabled their clients to consistently match or beat the performance of the popular market averages? Along the same lines, do you think that there would have been a veritable flood of money pouring into mutual funds and equity index funds if investors could obtain the same level of performance by working with a stockbroker? Finally, do you think that many of the major brokerage firms would encourage their brokers to direct funds from wealthy clients to investment management firms if the brokers could provide investment advice to clients that would match or beat the performance of those managers?

I've never seen a brokerage firm advertisement that documented the fact that their overall research recommendations beat the performance of any of the popular market averages. If that sort of documentation was available and was advertised, my guess is that unsolicited telephone calls would be reversed. Rather than brokers calling prospective clients, prospective clients would be calling brokers.

Through all of the changes that have occurred in the investment industry over the years–along with the dramatic changes that are occurring now and will be occurring in the months and years ahead–two truisms have survived and will continue to survive:

1. Individuals invest in the stock market with the aim and the hope of at least matching the rates of return of the broad-based market averages–such as the Dow Jones Industrial Average or the Standard & Poor 500 Index. Historically the stock market–as measured by these popular averages–has provided investors with a rate of return that is much higher than most other investment alternatives.

2. It doesn't appear to matter whether investors make their own stock selections (active investors), are guided by their stockbrokers (active investors) or whether they have handed their money over to professional investment management firms or mutual funds (passive investors). There is ample evidence that most

individual investors have been frustrated in their efforts to match or beat the performance of the market.

I originally entered the brokerage business in 1966 and spent most of the next 20 years with some of the largest brokerage firms in the U.S. I left the business in 1985 primarily because of my own frustrations in not being able to consistently increase my clients' wealth. After a hiatus of roughly ten years, I re-entered the business in 1996. In contrast to my prior brokerage experience, this time I was employed by a small regional brokerage firm. There was no research department, hence discovering investment opportunities was entirely up to me. It's difficult, if not impossible, for anyone to build a business in the brokerage business unless they can demonstrate an ability to discover a steady flow of profitable investment ideas. I failed in that effort and was fired within a year because I didn't generate enough commissions for my firm.

There's something about getting fired that stirs one's competitive juices. A passion was aroused within me. I wanted to prove that it was possible for me–or for any average individual investor–to discover profitable investment ideas without depending on the research department of a full-service brokerage firm. Even in 1997 there were clear indications that there was an increasing amount of investment information becoming available on the Internet. That bolstered my confidence. In fact, the Internet was to become the primary source in my search for profitable investment ideas. However, I wasn't sure how one could demonstrate the effectiveness of using that information to make profitable investment decisions.

There was an additional challenge that had to be solved. Most individual investors have grown very dependent on the guidance and recommendations provided by their brokers. Even if an effective methodology for tapping into the resources of the Internet to discover investment opportunities could be developed, it would be unwise for individual investors to abruptly end their brokerage relationships and begin making independent investment decisions. There had to be a period of time dedicated to learning. They had to achieve a level of confidence that they could successfully discover profitable investment ideas *without* risking any of their own money.

A concept finally evolved that solved both of these challenges. That concept is a fantasy portfolio, and that's what this book is all about. At the end of April 1997, I gave myself $250,000 fantasy dollars to begin this experiment. I had never attempted anything like this, so there were no expectations. The only reason to think that this effort might lead to success was that the Internet was spawning an increasing number of sites that offered valuable investment information.

Knowing that if my efforts met with success, there would have to be impeccable records to demonstrate that performance, I established and diligently adhered to the financial controls that are discussed in Chapter 5. Every transaction from day one has been recorded. In addition, each of the five conditions cited at the beginning of Chapter 5 have been faithfully followed.

For the first two years I had just one primary method for discovering investment opportunities. I searched for companies that generated some of the financial profiles of companies that had epitomized growth, like Intel, Microsoft, Cisco and Dell. Using that method during the first two years, the performance of my fantasy portfolio almost consistently beat the weekly and monthly performance of the NASDAQ Composite (an index for stocks traded in the over-the-counter market). The first year's gain was slightly more than 100%, and that performance was repeated again in the second year, with the result that the original $250,000 grew to a bit more than $1 million by the end of the second year. During that same period of time, the NASDAQ Composite increased 54.5% the first year and 36.0% the second year.

During the first quarter of 1999 I discovered two sources of information on the Internet that contributed to a dramatic increase in the portfolio's performance throughout the third year. By the final week of 1999–after approximately 32 months of managing my fantasy portfolio–it had increased in value to over $5 million. And, in the first quarter of 2000, the value of the portfolio increased to over $10 million. Those two sources are identified in Chapter 3.

I didn't start this experiment with the intent of subsequently writing a book. However, the success that I experienced convinced me that others might benefit from the sources of information and methods that I used. More than anything, this book is intended as a guide for learning how to discover emerging growth stocks. That's what success in investing is all about…discovery. If you follow the recommended procedures presented in this book you will learn how to become an early discoverer of these emerging growth stocks. The knowledge and confidence that you will gain with your own fantasy portfolio will ultimately enable you to venture into the real world of investments and to be very successful in that world!

Chapter 1

The Times They Are A-Changing

In music, and in everything, the times they are a-changing. A new age is upon us and no one can halt its progress. Unlike revolutions of the past, however, the opportunity to share more fully in the largesse of this revolution is huge. Aspects of this new age already exist; the rest is being born daily. Amid the apparent chaos of change, there are rhythms at work, and patterns are beginning to emerge.

We are at the dawn of an Age of Networked Intelligence—an age that is giving birth to a new economy, a new politics, and a new society. Businesses will be transformed, governments will be renewed, and individuals will be able to reinvent themselves—all with the help of the new information technology.

The Digital Economy, by Dan Tapscott…Introduction, page 2.

The ultimate objective of all investors is to increase their wealth. There are a lot of philosophies about how wealth can be increased by investing in the stock market. This book presents just one philosophy. It's about increasing wealth by investing in emerging growth stocks. That word–*emerging*–probably needs some clarification. When used throughout this book it refers to any company that is about to embark on a sustained period of rapid revenue growth. In almost all instances, rapid revenue growth can be attributed to one of two developments: Either a company has developed a new product for an existing or modified market, or a new market has been discovered for an existing or modified product. The common element of both situations is that there is something new.

Two steps are required to be successful when investing in emerging growth stocks.

The first step involves discovery…finding future growth stocks early. All over America there are companies–large and small, young and old–that are about to embark on a rapid path of revenue growth. The majority of these companies haven't yet been discovered by Wall Street. More important, they have not yet been discovered by the nationwide–perhaps worldwide–universe of investors. You may not be the initial discoverer of any of these emerging growth companies, but using the methods described in this book you can become aware of these discoveries sooner than most other investors. In other words, it is possible to learn about these investment opportunities when their market values are still comparatively low.

The second step involves timing…deciding *when* to make your investment. Have you ever made an investment in a company that you knew was on the verge of dramatically growing their revenues…and then watched the market value of its stock do nothing for weeks, months or even years? It's very possible to be too early when investing in emerging growth stocks. We all tend to think that since we made the discovery, then all investors must know about the company. That simply is not true.

Until other investors become as convinced as you are of the exciting investment potential of the company that you've discovered, the market performance of that stock is likely to be lackluster. Two things happen when other investors share your discovery and your optimistic outlook. First, existing investors in that company become increasingly reluctant to sell their stock, resulting in a diminishing supply of stock available for other investors to buy. Second, a growing number of investors–individual as well as institutional–decide that they want to own the stock, resulting in an increasing demand for the stock. With increasing demand and decreasing supply, there is only one way that the price for that stock can go, and that is up!

Unless an emerging growth company is domiciled in one's own city or town, it will be very difficult for most average investors to become an initial discoverer of this type of investment opportunity. However, Chapter 3 will offer two specific methods that will enable anyone to spot these opportunities early on.

For now, let's take a look at the information dissemination process. This has been one of the primary wellsprings of wealth creation on Wall Street and throughout the investment industry. The folks on Wall Street don't have any better methods for discovering emerging growth stocks that you or me. However, an emerging growth stock will seldom soar in market value unless and until it has become known on Wall Street. Aware of that, many discoverers of emerging growth stocks will share their discovery with others and ultimately the discovery is brought to the attention of someone who works on the Street.

Why is Wall Street so important? The answer is that the folks on Wall Street have developed a wonderfully effective information distribution system. With networks of brokerage offices throughout the country, news of an emerging growth company discovery can be disseminated to investors nationwide within a matter of hours or days. That network represents a very powerful source of demand creation–as well as one of the principal sources of wealth building for the folks on Wall Street. As will be seen later, it also represents the key area of Wall Street that is most threatened by the Internet. For now, it's sufficient to mention that the Internet has the potential to disseminate information faster and to a wider audience than Wall Street's network of brokerage offices.

A Primer on Brokerage Firms

There are basically three types of brokerage firms: Full-service, Discount and Online. The essential difference–from an average investor's point of view–between a full-service brokerage firm and the other two is that full-service brokerage firms have research departments. They hire analysts who study industries and companies and then issue recommendations to investors based upon their analyses. Included in this category would be firms like Merrill Lynch, A.G. Edwards, Lehman Bros., etc. Discount and online brokerage firms do not have research departments. The one thing that full-service brokerage firms and discount brokerage firms have in common is that each employs stockbrokers. Charles Schwab is perhaps the best known of discount brokerage firms. Because commission rates charged by discount brokerage firms are substantially lower than those levied by full-service firms, stockbrokers at the discount firms tend to earn less money than their full-service counterparts. Online brokerage firms do not have stockbrokers, a fact that enables them to charge the lowest commissions of the three. E-trade and Ameritrade are two examples of online brokers.

The fastest growing of these three categories is the online brokerage firm category. The growth of these firms has been so dramatic within the past couple of years that some pundits have suggested that in the not too distant future they will be the giants of the investment industry. That may or may not come true. Remember the first sentence of this chapter? If the full-service brokerage firms–with their higher commission charges–can help their clients to increase their wealth, those higher commission charges become irrelevant and their clients will be disinclined to shift their accounts to online or discount brokerage firms. The higher commission charges become relevant *only* when clients become aware that their investment performances with full-service brokerage firms have been below-average–average being defined as the performance of such market indices as the Dow Jones Industrial Average (DJIA) or the Standard and Poor 500 Index (S&P 500).

On the other hand, the rock-bottom commissions charged by online brokerage firms are equally irrelevant if there is no concomitant growth of their clients' wealth. Given a choice between low commissions/below-average performance and high commissions/above-average performance, any intelligent investor will opt for the latter. Therefore, it is implausible to think that the majority of investors will convert from the full-service brokerage firms to the world of online investing–unless and until they discover a method of investing that will enable them to at least beat the performances that they experienced with the full-service brokerage firms.

The truth is that many individual investors have been delivering a message about performance for quite some time. The huge growth of assets flowing into mutual funds during the past decade is a clear indication that the analysts/ brokers of full-service brokerage firms have not been doing a very good job of increasing their clients' wealth. When stock mutual funds also failed to deliver satisfactory performance, the industry witnessed a huge influx of assets into index funds. Investors did their talking with their money. If the professionals–stockbrokers, investment advisors, mutual fund managers, etc.–couldn't provide performance that at least mirrored the performance of the market, many investors decided to fire them! The message was simple: Why pay commissions and fees for inferior performance?

At the core of this fundamental problem is the following quote:

> *Give a man a fish and you feed him for a day.*
> *Teach him how to fish and you feed him for a lifetime.*
> Author Unknown

Full-service brokerage firms have succeeded in creating a system wherein investors have become highly dependent on them for investment guidance. In other words, they were successful in "feeding investors for a day." Since individual investors were not taught "how to fish"–or how to make their own investment decisions–they continued to look for better alternatives, none of which enabled them to become independent of the financial professionals.

My basic premise is that investors can successfully be taught "how to fish" for a lifetime. If this premise is valid, then there is no question about the probability that online brokerage firms will continue to grow more rapidly than the other two types of brokerage firms. As recently as four or five years ago, this learning process probably would not have been possible. Today it is possible. The enabling mechanism for this learning process is the Internet…along with an effective, risk-free learning system that is detailed Chapter 3.

A Brief History of Online Brokerage Firms

The first online brokerage firm (K. Aufhauser & Co., now Ameritrade) appeared in 1994. As recently as early 1997 there were fewer than 20 online brokerage firms. By mid-1998 there were more than 70 such firms, and less than a year later there were more than 100.

The number of investors using the Internet to execute their trades has experienced similarly impressive growth. According to International Data Corporation (IDC), at the end of 1997 there were 3.5 million online investment accounts. By the end of 1998, that number had swelled to 6.4 million. It has been estimated that one of every five individual investors now has an online brokerage account. IDC projects that these numbers will grow to 10.1 million by the end of 1999, 14.4 million by 2000, 19.3 million by 2001 and 24.7 million by the end of 2002.

The possibility that the online brokerage industry might continue its rapid growth received a huge dose of credibility on June 1, 1999 when the largest full-service brokerage firm in the world–Merrill Lynch–announced that it would offer its clients the opportunity to trade online. Many analysts believe that Merrill's decision will have the same impact on the online brokerage business as the May 1, 1975 S.E.C. mandate to abolish fixed rate commissions. The latter decision gave birth to the discount brokerage industry, pioneered by Charles Schwab.

What is the engine driving the growth of the online brokerage industry? According to a report from Jupiter Communications, a leading consultant and market research firm that focuses on the Internet, the allure of online trading can be explained by three primary benefits to investors: lower commissions (45%), convenience (36%) and control (12%).

Consider the following: The commission for a buy or sell order executed with an online brokerage firm over the Internet may cost anywhere from $5 to $20, *regardless* of the number of shares involved in the trade or the dollar value of each share traded. That same trade executed through a full-service brokerage firm might cost $100 to $200–or *higher, depending on* the number of shares involved and the dollar value of each share traded.

That may seem like a "no-brainer" decision for most investors. However, the following thoughts offer some explanation as to why more investors have not responded to the lure of lower transaction costs offered by online brokers and have remained with their full-service brokers.

Inertia.

The underlying thought here is that time-tested expression, "If it ain't broke, don't fix it!" In 1995 the stock market–as measured by the Standard & Poor 500 Index (S&P 500)–gained 37.6%. In 1996, the gain was 23.0%, in 1997 the gain was 33.4%, in 1998 the gain was 26.7% and in 1999 the gain was 19.5%. If an individual had investments that matched the performance of the S&P 500 during that five-year period, his/her investments *more than tripled* (+241.8%)!

Putting those percentages into dollar amounts might be more impressive: $10,000 invested at the beginning of 1995 would have grown to $34,180 by the end of 1999. Even if an investor achieved just half of those gains, he/she would probably be complacent since one of the most popular alternatives to investing in the stock market–Certificates of Deposit (CDs)–was hovering around a yield of roughly 5% during those five years.

Lack of Perceived Value.

In the history of any new technology–and clearly the Internet represents a new technology for most of us–there is usually a sequential acceptance of the technology by different groups of consumers. This pattern is illustrated in Geoff Moore's book *Inside the Tornado.*

The first group to accept a new technology is what Moore calls the Innovators. They are the technology enthusiasts. They're not sure whether or not a market will exist for the new technology, but they believe that sooner or later it will have a beneficial impact on their lives. In the world of investing, these folks were probably already doing their own research. They didn't need the guidance provided by the analysts and stockbrokers of the full-service brokerage firms. When online trading became available, they enthusiastically embraced the opportunity to benefit from lower transaction costs.

Moore refers to the second group as Early Adopters, or Visionaries. These people are revolutionaries of a sort. They believe that a new technology has the potential to make a break with the customary processes of the past and to create an entirely new future. From an economic point of view, they believe that being among the first to embrace a new technology will give them a unique–perhaps insurmountable–competitive advantage over the old order. In the world of investments, these folks were probably among the first to discover some of the new sources of investment information on the Internet. Once they learned how to use that information profitably, they joined the ranks of online clients.

The third group is comprised of Pragmatists. They differ from the previous two groups in that they are neutral about the benefits of technology. However, once the benefits of the new technology have achieved a proven track record of useful productivity improvement they are willing to accept it. Usually a strong recommendation from people they trust will accelerate their acceptance. Investors who have not yet discovered the sources of investment information on the Internet–or who have discovered those sources but have not yet learned how to use that information profitably–continue to do business with the full-service brokerage firms. They need the investment guidance provided by their personal relationship with a stockbroker.

Moore labels the fourth group as the Late Majority or Conservatives. These folks are usually pessimistic about their ability to gain any value from new technologies and they accept them reluctantly. Why then, do they accept them at all? Because they become convinced that the rest of the world is going to pass them by if they don't! These folks probably haven't even begun to explore the possibility of discovering investment ideas on the Internet. Therefore it will probably be at least a year or two before they become potential clients for the online brokerage firms.

Moore refers to the fifth group as Laggards or Skeptics. During the Industrial Revolution these folks were referred to as Luddites. They cling to the past with a fervor that almost precludes any possibility of their accepting a new technological advancement. They spend their energies researching for reasons to reject any technology that threatens their "status quo". These folks are a stockbroker's dream come true. It will probably be many years before they consider the possibility of opening an online brokerage account.

It should be mentioned that there are some individual investors who don't fit into any of these categories. These folks are so busy pursuing successful careers in business or one of the professions that they simply don't have time to explore the potential benefits of online trading. However, rather than be categorized as Luddites, these folks are more likely to search out and work with a broker or financial advisor who has learned how to discover profitable investment ideas on the Internet.

Concern about Security.

In spite of the fact that providing confidential financial information over the Internet is no riskier than handing a waiter your credit card, many individual investors view online trading with skepticism. According to experts, this skepticism is unwarranted.

Nevertheless, the concerns that many individuals have about the security of opening an online account are real. I asked my son to review and critique the early manuscript for this book. He's a lawyer for a satellite communications company, so he has an above-average comprehension of technology. His comments regarding the risk of online trading were very revealing to me:

> *I was scared, really scared the first time (I opened an account). When you go to a bank, you give them money and while they don't give you a loaf of bread or a box of widgets in return, they at least give you a piece of paper memorializing the transaction. Trading online you get zippo. You click a button, commit yourself to paying thousands of dollars with NOTHING to show for it. Don't underestimate this!! This is an extremely intimidating barrier for people to overcome."*

Conversation with my son.

My initial response to this is that online brokerage firms have to comply with the same rules and regulations promulgated by the SEC that discount and full-service brokerage firms must comply with. In addition, they offer the same SIPC account insurance that the discount and full-service firms offer.

However, I think that the overarching consideration for all investors who are contemplating opening an online account is this: The potential growth for online brokerage firms is enormous. It's not much of a stretch to imagine that some day they will be the "giants" of the investment world, just as Amazon.com has emerged from an obscure, newborn company into one of the giants of the book-selling industry.

But that potential is predicated on their ability to "get it right" today. Losing or misplacing investors' funds or making errors in the execution of clients' orders would almost certainly preclude any online firms guilty of those transgressions from participating in the potentially exhilarating growth that lies ahead.

Finally, some comfort can be derived from the fact that making a decision to open an online account today is not as risky as it might have been just two years ago. Why? Because there are approximately ten million investors who have already successfully tested the waters and preceded you into the world of online investing.

Need for Guidance.

In my opinion, this is the most compelling reason most investors have for continuing their relationship with a full-service brokerage firm. The average investor assumes that his/her broker knows more than he does or she does about the forces that determine market values. After all, a broker–like a doctor or lawyer or any other professional–is intensely focused on his/her profession daily, throughout the year. Because of that focus we expect that a professional will bring a higher level of expertise to our investment decisions and that this higher level of expertise will result in better investment performance than what we could achieve on our own.

However, I would suggest that the need for guidance is more deeply rooted than simple reliance on the expertise of a financial advisor. There are over 6,000 companies whose stock is publicly traded on the New York Stock Exchange (NYSE), the American Stock Exchange (ASE) or with the National Association of Securities Dealers (NASD). There has to be some sort of intelligent filtering system to help individual investors in their selection process. The full-service brokerage firms provide that filtering system with the research done by analysts and with the guidance of individual brokers. To be sure, there are some serious conflicts of interest with both analysts and brokers, but for most clients of full-service brokerage firms it's the only filtering system that they know and trust.

A lot of the information provided by analysts is not yet available on the Internet–in particular, their detailed research reports. Even though those research reports are noticeably absent, there is currently a plethora of valuable investment information available on the Internet that can help in the search for profitable investment ideas. In fact, investors who learn how to access and use these information sources on the Internet can achieve above-average investment performance without access to the reports from analysts.

However, there is a high probability that analysts' research reports will soon be available on the Internet. In fact, there seems to be a compelling opportunity for Internet sites that offer pure investment research, totally independent and uncluttered by conflicting relationships with full-service brokerage firms. There is currently at least one home page on the Internet that fits that profile. There will undoubtedly be more.

One possibility for pure research sites might be entrepreneurial analysts breaking away from full-service brokerage firms. If the analysts on this team have impeccable performance credentials and if they are resolutely committed to providing honest, insightful information to individual investors, their Internet site could be financially supported by either advertisements or subscriptions. The key to both the cost of the subscription and the probability of their longevity would be their ability to discover profitable investment opportunities for their subscribers.

Another source might be consulting firms that provide marketing analyses for corporate clients. Some of the research that they perform for the corporate clients might be re-packaged as a valuable source of information for individual investors, thereby opening a new source of revenues for the consulting firms.

What all of this clearly suggests is that soon all individual investors will no longer have to rely on the research generated by full-service brokerage firms to guide their investment decisions. This means that the only remaining motivation for investors to remain with full-service brokerage firms will be the guidance provided by the personal relationship between client and stockbroker. This begs the question, "Can individual investors acquire enough investment knowledge and experience to make the stockbroker relationship redundant?"

Becoming Your Own Broker

Based upon my experience as a stockbroker with full-service brokerage firms, I'm convinced that collectively, stockbrokers and financial advisors are no more or less intelligent than the average individual investor.

What is it, then, that differentiates them from the rest of us? If we're intellectual peers, what is it that has enabled investment advisors to win our confidence? Why do we assume that they can make better investment decisions than we can make? Why are we so willing to respond to their investment recommendations?

I would suggest that there are two answers to these questions:

1. *Investment professionals are like most other professionals in that their skills are honed and fortified through repetition.* They make investment decisions many times a day throughout the year. Both their successful and unsuccessful decisions increase their investment knowledge.

   In contrast, most individual investors make investment decisions with a probable frequency ranging roughly from once a month to once a year. With that level of infrequency, it's very difficult to acquire even a basic knowledge of investing. Given the limited number of decisions being made, it's unrealistic for any individual to expect to acquire investment skills that could match the investment skills of a stockbroker, a mutual fund manager or an independent investment manager.

2.   The further advantage that investment professionals have is that *the decisions they make are usually for other people, using other people's money.* Hence, they aren't constrained the way most of us would be in making frequent investment decisions with our own money, which may result in the erosion of our wealth.

Investment advisors get paid for making recommendations or investment decisions for their clients. Successful investment advisors know that risk is an inherent component of investing and they try to educate their clients about this reality. The bottom line is that most investment advisors feel less inhibited about making investment recommendations or decisions with other people's money than most individual investors would feel with their own money.

Can individual investors acquire a higher level of knowledge and experience by:

1.   Increasing the frequency of their investment decisions; and
2.   Eliminating the risk of losing money?

The answer to both 1 and 2 is an emphatic "YES!" The two are inextricably related, but let's examine each individually.

1.   Using the system that will be detailed in Chapter 5, investors can make an unlimited number of investment decisions. In fact, increasing the number of decisions will enhance the learning process. Although there are no limits to the number of possible decisions, the research methods revealed in Chapter 3 provide effective and prudent limits to excessive decision-making. In fact, as progress is made with the research methods, the investment decisions will become increasingly difficult, which tends to intensify the learning process.

Incidentally, the disciplines recommended for this learning project are disciplines that many stockbrokers don't experience in the normal course of conducting their business. Consequently it's possible individuals pursuing the learning process outlined in this book can acquire some skill sets that have not been acquired by their brokers.

Although words like "discipline," "learning process" and "difficult" have been used to describe this experience, it should more accurately be viewed as "fun," "challenging" and "exciting." If you have competitive instincts and enjoy learning, you will eagerly embrace this program.

2. Increasing your investment skills by becoming an active investor with your own money (for example, making an investment decision at least once per week) might provide you with improved investment skills. However, the probability of losing money in the process is a risk that most investors are wisely unwilling to take.

Acquiring the necessary investment skills without risking personal wealth presents a dilemma for most investors. Their lower level of investment skills stems from lack of experience, or infrequency in making investment decisions. Gaining that experience by making frequent "buy" and "sell" decisions with real money is fraught with the considerable risk that the resulting financial losses could be significant.

The program outlined in Chapter 5 does not use real money. It uses "fantasy" money, so the risk of financial loss has been eliminated. Decisions can be made without the inhibiting consideration that money might be lost. Eliminating that fear enables you to be more dispassionate about making investment decisions. It also allows you to analyze both your successes and failures in a more realistic light, thereby providing you with a more accurate analysis, untainted by the emotions of fear and greed.

The emergence of the Internet as a valuable source of investment information makes this exercise particularly timely. The Internet is basically a tool, albeit a knowledge tool. Like any tool, its effectiveness is determined primarily by the skills of the person using the tool. These skills are best developed by repetition.

Investing is not unlike any other of life's pursuits in that skills aren't acquired simply by reading a book. For example, reading a book or several books about perfecting your golf swing is not likely to improve your score unless you get out on the course and put into practice what you have learned from the book. There is something about putting your feet to the fire that accelerates the development of skills. "How To" books can be very stimulating, but if that stimulation is purely intellectual without subsequent action or application, then skill levels are likely to remain unchanged. As with any learning adventure, experience and repetition are the best and surest way to build proficiency in the pursuit of investment skills.

Remember, this is a learning experience, totally unrelated to the level of real investment funds that you might currently have or that you will have in the future. It is designed to provide you with a level of repetitive decision making that will enhance the learning process, ergo, your investment skills. And, because you will be using fantasy money, you will enjoy the same lack of financial pressure enjoyed by stockbrokers. Like them, you will be learning with money that is not your own!

The amount of time required for this learning can be controlled entirely by you. As a guide, I would suggest that you commit as much time to the process as you currently commit to reading a daily newspaper or whatever magazines you read on a regular basis. You may discover–as I have–that scanning selected pages on the Internet is faster and more informative than perusing a daily newspaper or leafing through a magazine.

If you follow the recommended procedures in this book you will almost certainly increase your investment knowledge and your investment skills. Of course, once you succeed in increasing your ability to make profitable investment decisions, the eventual harvest will be an increase in your future investment returns–in other words, greater wealth for you!!

Chapter 2

Why the Changes Were Inevitable

*Market participants are human beings, after all, and are subject to the same impulses as anyone. Many emotions affect their decision-making process, but two sentiments have the most lasting impact–**fear** and **greed**. Investors in general are scared of losing money, and all are anxious to make more profits. These feelings become accentuated in the professional investor community, whose members are caught up in the treadmill of maintaining good short-term performance.*
Security Analysis on Wall Street, by Jeffrey C. Hooke, page 7

The Flow of Investment Information

Forward-looking investment information is the real currency of Wall Street. This is information that projects or attempts to estimate the future financial performance of the economy, various industry segments and individual companies. It's difficult to imagine how Wall Street–or more accurately, the full-service brokerage industry–could survive without access to, indeed, control of, the distribution and interpretation of this vital information.

The emergence of the Internet represents a potential competitive threat to Wall Street's control and distribution of this information. Consider the following quote by Lou Gerstner, CEO of IBM, taken from the lead, front-page story in the November 7, 1997 issue of *The Wall Street Journal*, entitled "High-End Brokers Will Shift to Net, IBM's Gerstner Says":

> *Your entire industry will move to the Net. Not just the discounters; all of you will. It was noteworthy that the IBM chief couldn't even provoke a big ripple of dissent from the veteran Wall Street crowd when he quoted the president of E*Trade Group Inc., an online trading firm, as saying "Stock-brokerage is not a profession you want your children to go into."*

Up to the present time, full-service brokerage firms have effectively controlled the flow of forward-looking investment information from publicly owned corporations to the investing public. The Securities and Exchange Commission (SEC)–the governmental agency with the mandate to protect the investing public–has given its tacit approval to this somewhat monopolistic control of investment information.

The SEC's tacit approval of the flow of information from companies through security analysts and then to the investing public suggests that the SEC considers analysts to be less naïve than the public and therefore less likely to be duped. Although the SEC encourages publicly owned companies to provide financial projections to investors, our legal system effectively dissuades these companies from doing so.

How? Any company found guilty of issuing untrue or incomplete information can be subject to harsh penalties. Because of the many imponderables involved in financial projections, actual results are sometimes lower than corporate management had previously projected. Rather than expose themselves to the risk of being found guilty of misleading the public, most corporations have opted to provide investment information–particularly information that provides a view of potential future financial performance–through analysts working for full-service brokerage firms.

Using their financial skills and industry knowledge, analysts interpret that information and distribute it orally or in written reports to institutional and individual investors. These reports typically contain a recommendation–such as "Buy" or "Hold"–concerning the timeliness of investing in the company featured in the report. However, most importantly, the typical research report includes future *earnings-per-share projections* for the company being analyzed.

Companies' earnings per share (EPS) ultimately determine stock market values. It used to be that earnings were important because, in almost all instances, earnings were the source of dividend payments. Dividend payments represented an investment alternative to interest payments from bond investments or to interest earned on bank deposits. That's no longer true. Although it remains true that earnings still represent a potential source of dividend payments, most investors today focus exclusively on earnings. Their psychology seems to be that a company should retain current earnings for internal investments that will promote future growth of revenues and earnings. Sustained quarterly increases in revenues and earnings usually result in higher stock market values. Higher stock market values have historically offered a higher rate of return to investors than dividend payments.

The relationship between the market value of a stock and the underlying company's earnings is commonly referred to as the price-to-earnings ratio–or more succinctly, the P/E ratio. Because of this ineradicable link between earnings per share and market values, investors gain a huge advantage by having access to an informed estimate of what future earnings might be. If you have a reliable estimate of what the future earnings might be and you can apply a reasonable P/E multiple to those earnings, you can project a future market value for the stock.

For example, let's assume that the market value of Company A is currently $30 per share. Company A's current fiscal year has just ended and they reported earnings of $2.00 per share. You recently read an analyst's report on Company A that projected earnings per share of $3.00 for the next fiscal year. You know that the company currently sports a 15 P/E ratio (market value of $30 divided by earnings of $2.00). Although any company that can sustain an EPS growth rate of 50% ($2.00 current fiscal year to $3.00 projected next fiscal year) deserves a higher P/E ratio than 15, you feel confident that at least the 15 P/E ratio is attainable. Therefore you can comfortably project a future market value of $45 per share ($3.00 earnings per share times 15 P/E ratio) or a rate of increase (rate of return on your investment) of 50% over the next year (current market value of $30, future market value of $45).

That's why estimated earnings are so important–if they're credible. And, in today's environment, they are available only from analysts working for full-service brokerage firms. Obviously then, control of this crucial investment information gives analysts an enormous amount of power and influence over the market value of the stocks which they follow.

Can Analysts Accurately Forecast Earnings?

An appropriate question at this point might be, "How can analysts be so knowledgeable about the future profitability of any corporation?" The probable answer is that aside from their acquired financial analytical skills they receive considerable guidance with their earnings forecasts from the most logical of sources, either the chief financial officers (CFOs) or the chief executive officers (CEOs) of the companies whose future earnings they are estimating.

After all, how can an analyst working outside of a corporation's walls be privy to such pertinent inside information as new order flow, expense reduction programs, new product/market opportunities, new financing requirements, etc., and convert those variables into earnings projections without receiving guidance directly from "the horse's mouth?" A logical follow-up question is "Why do corporate CEOs and CFOs provide guidance to analysts?"

Many executives of publicly owned companies probably wish that a better system for disseminating forward-looking investment information was available. To them, providing investment guidance through the analyst system represents a double-edged sword that can both benefit and damage their companies.

From a positive perspective, putting the focus on the analyst system represents a very efficient method for circulating financial projections and commentary to the universe of institutional and individual investors.

The potential negative is that enabling analysts to be the focal point for the flow of financial projections empowers those analysts with an inordinate amount of influence. The earnings per share projections become the principal determinant of present and future market values. When actual earnings per share fall short of those projected by analysts, the all too common consequence is that disappointed investors, especially institutional investors, sell their shares. This selling is exacerbated when analysts, who feel that the company has betrayed them, subsequently make lower earnings per share projections and also lower their investment recommendation on the stock.

For Now...A Mutually Beneficial Relationship

There is undoubtedly more than one answer to why corporate executives provide guidance to financial analysts, but one answer is indisputably paramount: Through their networks of nationwide branch offices, each staffed with individual brokers, full-service brokerage firms have created a marvelous investment information distribution system. In order to understand why this flow of investment information is so important to corporations, let's divert for a moment.

When a corporation sells stock to the public it essentially offers partial ownership of the corporation in exchange for investors' cash. Investors thereby acquire an ownership position in the corporation. As such, they have the right to vote for the corporation's board of directors who, in turn, choose the officers who will be responsible for the management of the corporation. Therefore, the "pecking order", at least in theory, becomes corporate officers accountable to the board of directors and the board of directors accountable to investors. Note that investors–in theory–have the ultimate corporate power in publicly owned corporations. In a perfect capitalistic system, it's the shareholders' interests that must be served. Robert Goizueta, the former CEO of Coca-Cola summed it up as follows:

> *Management does not get paid to make shareholders comfortable; we get paid to make shareholders rich.*
> http:www.investors.com/web-edition/today/leadersnsuccess.html

Most erudite CEOs will agree with Goizueta. This axiom dovetails neatly with one of the motivations to become an investor, which is to have the market value of one's investment increase over time. The market value of one's stock can increase only when the demand for that stock–investors wanting to own the stock - continues to exceed the supply–current owners of the stock willing to sell. There are many factors that can increase the demand, or decrease the supply, for a company's stock, but in the final analysis it is the ability of the company's management team to expand revenues and profits that increases shareholder value.

Sometimes the mere anticipation of growing revenues or growing earnings in the distant future will drive the price of a stock higher. In fact, there have been stocks that have soared in market value even though the underlying company had negative earnings (losses) and current revenues could best be described as modest. During the 1990s, many companies whose business was related to the Internet illustrated this phenomenon. The only logical explanation for this type of exuberant market price behavior is that there is a very high level of confidence that future revenues and earnings will be extraordinary.

How does Wall Street fit into this supply/demand picture? Wall Street's nationwide networks of stockbrokers have become a very effective force for influencing the demand for a company's stock. These stockbrokers are usually quite articulate and very persuasive in relating the investment merits of a company to potential investors. But, this answer raises a more important question, "How does the average stockbroker in Portland, Maine, acquire knowledge about the investment merits of a company in San Diego, California?"

In almost all situations, that communication begins with information flowing from the CEO or CFO of a publicly owned company to security analysts. If the information received by the analyst is likely to have a positive, or negative, impact on the price of the company's stock, it will first be passed on to the management of the brokerage firm that employs the analyst. Analysts then pass that information on to key institutional accounts. Finally, the information is disseminated to the nationwide network of stockbrokers via an internal broadcast system and/or a written report. The brokers then begin their selling campaign by contacting individual clients.

Note carefully the sequential flow of this information, specifically, which group of recipients is at the beginning of the flow of information and which group is at the end. If the information being cascaded through the system has considerable investment value, it can be assumed that the market value of the subject stock will steadily increase as each new group of investors receives the information.

More Than One Way to Increase the Bottom Line

Why would the management of a brokerage firm want to receive meaningful investment information from an analyst prior to parceling that information out to its customers, the individual and institutional investors?

A very important part of a full-service brokerage firm's profits comes from making a market in a stock–their trading operations. If they are about to issue a "buy" recommendation on a specific company, there are at least a couple of ways that the firm can profit from that recommendation. The most obvious way is from the commissions that are generated by their nationwide network of brokers who recommend the stock to their clients. As each client responds to the recommendation by buying the stock, a commission is generated for the broker and his/her firm. There is a less obvious, but equally important, way that profits are generated for the brokerage firm.

Knowing that their analyst's "buy" recommendation could significantly increase the demand for a stock, a brokerage firm would probably want to accumulate an inventory or supply of that stock. As their clients place orders to buy the stock, a brokerage firm can fill those orders in one of two ways. The first way is to go to the open market–be that the floor of an exchange or the over-the-counter market–and buy the stock for their clients. In return for this "shopping" for the client, they charge a commission.

The second way is to sell their client stock that has been previously purchased by the brokerage firm and placed in their inventory. This procedure is not unlike what any good merchant would want to do: buy merchandise at a reduced price, advertise the merchandise and then fill the demand from inventory, at a higher price than the cost of the inventory. This is a huge source of profits for most full-service brokerage firms.

Another profitable source of activity for some regional and nationwide full-service brokerage firms is to "make a market" for selected stocks that trade in the over-the-counter market. When a brokerage firm makes a market for a specific stock, it performs a function quite similar to that performed by a specialist on the New York Stock Exchange. Like the specialist, they provide "bid" and "asked" quotes on the stocks that they make a market in. The "bid" represents the price that investors (including the market makers) are willing to pay for the stock and the "asked" represents the price at which investors (including the market makers) are willing to sell the stock.

The advantage enjoyed by both the exchange specialists and market makers is that they are aware of open orders that have been placed away from the market. What do I mean by "away from the market?" Most investors place orders to buy or sell a stock "at the market," which means that when the order gets to the market it is filled immediately at the current bid or asked price. Other investors prefer to name the price at which they want to buy or sell a stock. Those orders are entered in the books of the specialist or market maker and remain "open" until the interaction of supply and demand meets at that specified price, at which time the open buy or sell order effectively becomes a market order.

This knowledge or awareness of open orders–the number of shares and the stated price at which investors are willing to buy or sell–empowers the specialist or the market maker to enter the market as a buyer or seller whenever an opportunity is spotted to make a profit. For example, every stock at any given point in time has a bid and asked price. The bid and asked prices are determined by open orders to buy and sell at specified prices that have been sent by investors' brokers to the specialist or the market maker. Absent any intervention by the specialist or market maker, buyers submitting market orders would pay the asked price–which is always higher than the bid price–and sellers submitting market orders would pay the bid price–which is always lower than the asked price.

For purposes of illustration, let's assume that a market order to buy is sent to a specialist. When the order reaches the specialist, the best open order to buy (the bid price) is $25 and the best open order to sell (the offer price) is $26. Again, without the specialist's intervention, this order would be filled at a price of $26 (the offer price). However, the specialist has the option of creating his own bid price for the stock. For example, he/she can enter a bid of $25.50. By increasing the bid by $0.50, he/she hopes to entice another investor to sell him stock at $25.50, rather than at $25, which was the price a seller would have received without the intervention of the specialist. If successful, the specialist could then sell the stock at $25.75 to the investor who submitted the market order to buy, which would be better than the offer price of $26. The specialist would pocket the $0.25 spread between the $25.50 that he paid to buy the stock and the $25.75 price at which he sold the stock.

Specialists or market makers can't compete with customer open orders. In other words, the specialist in this illustration had to buy the stock at a price higher than the existing open order to buy and he had to sell the stock at a price lower than the existing open order to sell. However, those $0.25 spreads over a period of days, weeks and months can amount to very substantial profits for these specialists and market makers.

To give you an idea about how important investment banking, asset management and trading activities are to a full-service brokerage firm, analysts estimate that in 1998 less than $2 billion of Merrill Lynch's revenue of $17.5 billion came from commissions paid by individual and insitutional investors for stock and bond trades.

The Inherent Risks of the Analyst System

Every three months, Wall Street throws an invitation-only dance called earnings season. On one side of the ballroom are the chief financial officers of companies that are about to report their earnings. On the other side are the analysts, whose job it is to guess those earnings. The dance comes to an end with the company usually announcing numbers that are amazingly close to what most of the analysts guessed.

From the point of view of the individual investor, this world seems about as real as Merlin's. Indeed, the predictive abilities of the analysts of Wall Street appear to be nothing less than magical, and individual investors often see the analysts as wizards, hunched over cauldrons of data, summoning a crystalline vision of the future.

The truth is a little bit more complicated. Analysts usually get their earnings predictions from hints dispensed by executives of the company being "analyzed." An average CEO has a good idea of what the quarterly earnings will be well before the end of the quarter and will pass that on—one way or another—to the analysts that cover the company.

Business Week, 10/5/98, **What Every Investor Should Know About Stock Analysis**

As mentioned earlier in this chapter, earnings-per-share projections have a powerful influence on stock market valuations. The onus for the accuracy of these projections has been shifted from corporations to the analysts covering specific companies. But remember, the financial benefits flowing to the brokerage firms employing these analysts is substantial. In spite of that benefit, the brokerage firms thus far have been immune to the legal and financial risks that companies would be liable to if these projections were announced publicly by the companies rather than through analysts.

In fact, about the only risk faced by the brokerage firms and their analysts is the risk to their reputation for predictive accuracy if projections fall short of performance. And therein lies one of the flaws of this system for distributing financial projections. If a company's actual earnings performance falls short of analysts' projections, analysts are very quick to lower the investment recommendation for that stock. Since so many investors–individual as well as institutional–follow analysts' recommendations in lemming-like fashion, the consequence of analysts' lowering their recommendations is often a precipitous decline in the market value of a company's stock.

Are earnings projections that important, particularly to institutional investors who are presumed to be more sophisticated and knowledgeable than individual investors? Every year Merrill Lynch polls its institutional clients to learn more about their investment strategies. The 1998 poll revealed the following:

> Among the 122 outfits that responded to Merrill's poll, the top strategy was buying stocks of companies that had just delivered higher than expected earnings and selling those whose earnings had fallen short. On Wall Street, these occurrences are known as 'earnings surprises.' As the accompanying table shows, this strategy played a role in the stock selection of 54% of the institutions.
>
> The conceit behind the 'earnings-surprise' approach is that winners are likely to keep on delivering, while companies whose profits fall short of Wall Street expectations will continue to have trouble. The popularity of this strategy goes a long way toward explaining why stocks get so severely punished after failing to meet expectations. http://interactive.wsj.com/edition/c...nt/articles/SB881373225563258000.htm

Whatever reasonable explanations might be offered by the company for the earnings shortfall, those explanations are likely to fall on deaf investor ears. The myopic focus on near-term quarterly earnings performance and the precarious interposition of analysts as the channel for disseminating financial projections has damaged the issuing company's reputation. It can take a long time for the market value of a company's stock to recover from this type of debacle.

The Merrill Lynch poll was noteworthy, not for what it contained but particularly for what it did not contain. Of the twenty-four financial characteristics that the institutional investor respondents mentioned as being of strategic importance, not one was relevant to *revenue growth*! Why is this omission significant? First of all, it further illustrates the tunnel vision focus on earnings that typifies the management of many companies in America today. Wall Street analysts reinforce that focus. While it is certainly desirable for companies to strive for internal operational efficiencies to pump up earnings per share, clearly there are limitations to the gains that can be obtained from that process. In contrast, an aggressive and intelligent search by management for new products and new markets that can expand revenues offers a better potential for earnings growth that can extend far into the future.

Permit me to offer a simple illustration. Two farmers each have 100 apple trees. Over time, each has researched methods for improving the number of apples produced by each tree. One farmer stubbornly persisted in trying to uncover methods to increase the yield of each tree even though each new efficiency method produced minimal incremental production. The other farmer decided that the best way to increase his income was to spend some of his profits by developing a new orchard of apple trees or an alternative crop, based upon his/her analysis of market dynamics. In the long run, which of the two would you think prospered the most?

Given the fragility of channeling earnings projections through the analyst system and the volatility that can ensue when earnings fall short of projections, it seems logical that it is only a matter of time before steps will be taken by corporate management to reduce the inherent risks of this process.

The Inherent Conflicts of the Analyst System

The analyst system has other deficiencies insofar as individual and institutional investors are concerned. These deficiencies are almost all related to conflicts regarding which master(s) the analyst really serves. After reading the following, it ought to be quite clear that individual and institutional investors are not the masters being served by the analyst system—in spite of those investors' almost irreplaceable reliance on that system.

> *The question for investors is: 'Can you trust your analyst?' Unfortunately, the answer is not very much. At the major Wall Street houses, every analyst has a potential conflict of interest. The 'Chinese Wall' that on paper still separates a firm's analysts from its investment bankers continues to crumble as analysts are encouraged to scout deals. The analyst's firm is either the investment banker for a company he or she is covering—or it's wooing the company for a piece of that juicy revenue stream.*
> Business Week, 10/5/98, **Wall Street's Spin Game**

The reason for the "Chinese Wall" mentioned in the above quote predates today's standards. In former years, investment bankers and analysts, although employed by the same firm, were not supposed to communicate with one another about the companies they researched. Investment bankers were primarily involved with helping companies to raise additional capital or to provide guidance with merger and acquisition activities. It was presumed, on the other hand, that analysts would approach companies with a different perspective. Their job was to gather information about a company that would help investors to make buy and sell decisions. The investment bankers were expected to represent and work for the benefit of publicly owned companies. The analysts were expected to represent and work for the benefit of individual and institutional investors.

The investment banking activities of a brokerage firm require it to gather detailed and comprehensive financial information about a company that would normally be considered "inside" information not widely available to the investing public. This information is vitally important when considering a public offering of stock or counseling a company regarding merger or acquisition activities. In fact, the investment bankers have some of the same fiduciary responsibilities, and require the same in-depth financial information, that commercial bankers have when they make decisions about extending loans.

Any investor or investment advisor with access to that kind of information would possess a significant, and probably illegal, advantage insofar as investment decisions were concerned. In addition, an issuing company would not want that information widely distributed because it could jeopardize its competitive position within its industry. The imaginary "Chinese Wall" was created with the expectation that this sensitive information would be available *only* to the investment banking division of a brokerage firm.

If the above explains what used to be–perhaps what still ought to be–then why has it changed? Why has the analyst system pre-empted the investment banking system? Why are analysts now more important to a full-service brokerage firm than investment bankers? *The Wall Street Journal*, in a front page article on May 18, 1998 entitled "Today, Delivering Good News Is a Way To Ensure Good Business Relationships" provides answers to those questions:

> *Research analysts traditionally act as a filter between the stock market and investors. For years, these analysts toiled in relative obscurity, writing reports on companies or industries, making earnings forecasts and recommending which stocks investors should buy or sell.*
>
> *All that has changed in the 1990s. The boom on Wall Street–as securities firms advise corporate America in record numbers on mergers and initial public stock offerings–has transformed*

*many analysts' roles. Instead of simply assessing stocks, ana-
lysts increasingly promote them. The lure is great: If analysts
aggressively tout a company's stock, their firm stands a greater
chance at snaring an advisory role, and the fat fees that follow.
Now, analysts can be stars, receiving bonuses of several hundred thousand dollars for big underwriting deals. Bash a stock,
and your firm could be shut out.*

*The upshot: Many analysts now focus on helping bring in
investment banking deals. Independent stock picking is out the
window. This evolution has picked up steam in recent years
because when stocks seem only to rise, the value of fundamental analysis falls. And so, marketing stocks, where analysts help
investment bankers be cheerleaders for companies their firms
want to do business with, is where the action is.*

The very clear implication of all of this is that most analysts, formerly
viewed as representing individual and institutional investors, have now
evolved to the point where their primary concern is winning lucrative
investment banking deals from publicly owned companies. The benefi-
ciaries of this evolution–in addition to the analysts–are the full-service
brokerage firms that employ the analysts. Who are the losers? It would
be difficult to escape the conclusion that individual and institutional
investors, who rely on the analyst system for investment guidance, have
been sacrificed.

Even when analysts have not been tainted by the lure of investment
banking deals, there are inherent conflicts of interest within the analyst
system that constrain their ability or willingness to provide useful financial information to investors. Some of these constraints are as follows:

It's very difficult for an analyst to offer negative comments about
a company, even when those comments are warranted. Negative
comments might preclude an analyst's firm from participating in
an investment banking deal. More important, negative
comments from an analyst might result in losing access to

company executives, not being invited to company meetings for analysts and institutional investors and/or being denied access to the earnings "guidance" chats between top executives and analysts which are so critical for generating earnings forecasts.

Part of an analyst's compensation is determined by the amount of business that is generated by the analyst for his firm's trading desk. A "buy" recommendation for a company that was not previously followed by an analyst will generate a lot more profit for his firm than will a "sell" recommendation. Why? Sell recommendations just generate commissions. Buy recommendations offer the possibility for larger profits if the firm acquires an inventory of the stock prior to recommending it.

A "sell" recommendation from an analyst might also offend mutual funds that have a large position in that specific stock. If the sell recommendation results in a decline of the market value of that stock, the net asset value of a mutual fund might also decline, resulting in lower fees being earned by the mutual fund. More important, it might have an impact on the mutual fund's performance, which would result in a deterioration of the investor supply/demand factors. Since mutual funds represent such an enormous source of investment activity, most full-service brokerage firms try to avoid alienating them.

In view of all of these biases and conflicts of interest within the analyst system, the mother lode of the full-service brokerage firms, anyone doing business with one of these firms might want to re-evaluate his/her commitment. At the very least, investors should be aware of these conflicts of interest. This awareness will help to put analyst recommendations in a clearer light. There is ample evidence that–within the full-service brokerage firms–individual investors are often at the tail end of the investment information distribution system.

In most instances, receiving investment information well beyond its half-life results in diminished investment returns. One of the virtues of searching for investment information on the Internet is that you have the opportunity to discover investment information before it begins to lose value, thereby enhancing the possibility of higher investment returns.

If you're an individual investor who relies on the investment recommendations of a full-service brokerage firm, then being forewarned is being forearmed. You may not be getting the quality of investment guidance that you should reasonably expect.

Chapter 3

Doing Your Own Research

"Technology is the all-star of the New Era. Ideas and innovations are always the source of increasing wealth. Whether it is with steam shovels or satellite phone systems, by learning to make more with less, share information faster, or just invent new things, technology is the driving force behind all economic advancement. Today's technology, however, is different than that of the past. The networked economy, driven by advances in computers and telecommunications, has created an astounding opportunity. Information, capital, and new ideas travel at the speed of light across fiber-optic cables and, as a result, the era of increasing returns has replaced the era of diminishing returns. Competition has become global and efficiency has become the password to the secret of business survival."
Ibid, p. 77

In mid-1999, Jon Markman of MSN MoneyCentral conducted a workshop for investors in Las Vegas. He asked if any in the audience could name the top four performing stocks of the 1990s. Before reading further, what four stocks would you name? Here they are, along with the percentage increase in value for each:

Company	% Increase
Dell Computer	56,000
America Online	45,785
Cisco Systems	32,207
EMC	31,597

Those percentages don't mean an awful lot to most of us, so let's translate them into dollars. A $10,000 investment in Dell Computer on January 1, 1990, was worth $5.6 million at the time of Markman's workshop! To put those numbers into perspective, let's take a look at some companies that most of us would have picked as the top performers of the '90s:

Company	% Increase
Microsoft	6,190
Intel	2,350
Coca Cola	690
General Electric	670
Dow Jones Industrial Average	285
S&P 500	272

We can all play the game of "What if" by imagining how different our lives would be if we had invested in any of the top four performing stocks of the 1990s. It's a little like reading about people who have won a lottery–it provides us with a vicarious thrill! This chapter is all about improving the likelihood that you will discover stocks that have that type of potential for extraordinary growth. You may not discover another Dell, America Online, Cisco or EMC–but you might!

I can promise you this: Your chances of making such a discovery are significantly better using the methods detailed in this chapter than pursuing the same old investment methods that you've used in the past. There's another statement that I can make: If, at the beginning of 1990, you had been using the two systems that are offered in this chapter, you almost certainly would have discovered all four of those stocks.

Let me state very clearly what you will not learn from this chapter. You will not learn how to successfully invest in some of the largest corporations in America, like AT&T, IBM, General Motors, etc. Quite simply, in the competition to discover useful investment information about the giants of American industry, I don't know how any individual investor can gain a meaningful advantage over larger institutional investors. I do agree that the stocks of these larger corporations have a place in every individual's portfolio. However, I would suggest that investing in an index fund is the least complicated and lowest risk method for investing in those giant companies.

There's a very pragmatic reason why your research should be focused on smaller growth companies–there are a lot more of them! In late 1999 I did a search for companies that satisfied the following requirements:

Total revenues were at least $50 million.

Revenues increased by 40% or better, current year versus previous year.

Net Profit margins were at least 15% of Revenues.

The search produced a total of 167 companies that met those parameters. The following chart indicates how those companies were categorized based upon total revenues for the year. Notice that as the upper limit of revenues increased, the number of companies that qualify for that particular category decreased.

Annual Revenues	# of Companies
Less than $250 million	109
More than $250 million	58
Less than $500 million	141
More than $500 million	26
Less than $1 billion	156
More than $1 billion	11
Less than $5 billion	165
More than $5 billion	2

By the way, the only two companies that qualified in the *more than $5 billion* revenue category were America Online and Cisco! The results of this search demonstrate a point that Markman brought out in his seminar: "The secret to catching fish is to drop your line where the fish are!"

In the future you may discover your own sources for discovering budding growth stocks, but for now this chapter will identify two methods that will provide you with a daily flow of potential investment candidates. Using these two methods you will have no problem at all in selecting the original 15 stocks for your fantasy portfolio.

It's very important that you clearly understand that you're not going to learn very much by just picking 15 stocks from a list, or periodically eliminating one of the 15 stocks in your portfolio and replacing it with a new stock without doing any further research. The real learning occurs when you analyze why each new stock idea came to your attention in the first place. Something happened–a trigger event, if you will–that caused that stock to appear on your radar screen. Your challenge is to learn as much as possible about the company using the steps outlined later in this chapter. The purpose of that research is to help you determine the likelihood that the "trigger event" was a genuine harbinger of future above-average performance.

As you identify and get enthused about new discoveries, your thinking will be challenged by the dilemma of which stocks to remove from your portfolio to make room for the new discoveries. Remember that you can never have more than 15 stocks in the portfolio at any one time. Initially you might experience a very rapid turnover in your portfolio as you push out one of the old stocks to make room for one of the new. High initial turnover should not be viewed as being unusual nor should it have any negative implications. In fact, if you keep all of the original 15 stocks in your portfolio for more than a month, you're probably not doing a very good job of following the recommended procedures. Some of you will begin replacing a few of your original selections within the first couple of days. From my perspective, that would be a good sign that you're actively involved in the discovery/learning process.

The Long Path for the Discovery Process

Outstanding investment opportunities can be found at almost any point in time in most industry segments. However, it's usually easier to find companies with above-average growth potential in industries that offer the potential for above-average growth. Reading publications like *The Wall Street Journal, Investor's Business Daily, Barron's, Business Week* and *Fortune* can help you to identify industries with exceptional growth potential. For example, the January 11, 1999 issue of *Business Week* had a feature article entitled Industry Outlook (p. 88). It offered projected 1999 revenue growth rates for 21 separate industry groups. The following were the top five industry groups:

Computers & Chips	15.36%
Securities	10%
Software	6%
Telecommunications	4%
Autos	4%

Note that three of the top five–computers and chips, software and telecommunications–are directly involved with the information technology industry. In fact, it could have been argued that much of the growth in the securities industry would come from the trading activity in information technology stocks and from investment firms that offer online trading, a sub-segment of the information technology industry. What makes these growth rates even more alluring is the fact that the consensus for the overall growth of the economy at the beginning of 1999 was only 1.9%! The similar forecast for economic growth in 2000 was 3.6%. To put those growth rates in perspective, under normal conditions the overall economy will typically grow about 3% per year–in a robust economy it may grow 3% to 5%.

If the above projections had any validity, the compelling forecast for the computer and chips industry (a growth rate 50% higher than the #2 rated industry!) suggested that searching for stocks within that industry would offer the greatest opportunity for discovering potential winners. The *Business Week* industry forecast for the year 2000 was less specific. It simply projected the four leading industry groups: Computers, Software, Telecom and Securities. Although lacking specifics, the 2000 forecast is still of great value to investors. When you invest in companies within strong industry segments it's comparable to sailing with the wind at your back.

After you've identified an industry segment (or more) that has clear leadership characteristics, start searching for companies within that segment. Where do you find companies that can be categorized within an industry segment? One of the best sources can be found at the following Internet site: http://quote.yahoo.com/.

In the "Research" section, click on *By Industry*. This will bring you to an extensive list of industry categories: http://biz.yahoo.com/research/indgrp/.

Just for purposes of illustration, click on the *Telecommunications* industry. Notice that there are two sub-segments of this industry, *Equipment* and *Services*. Click on *Equipment* and you will get a listing of companies that manufacture equipment for the telecommunications industry. These companies are ranked based upon the consensus of recommendations issued by analysts who follow those companies.

Later in the chapter we will discuss in greater detail how you can systematically dig deeper for more information about the companies that you've discovered. For now, what you have unearthed with just a few clicks of your computer mouse is a pretty good list of potential companies for your portfolio.

Another useful method for securing the names of companies within a specific industry is to search the Internet for trade magazines that target that industry. How can you find those trade magazines? The following page of Yahoo! is a perhaps the best source: http://dir.Yahoo.com/Business_and_Economy/Magazines/Trade_Magazines/.

My area of interest has been the information technology industry. It probably took a couple of years, but I've accumulated a number of magazines that I've found to be useful sources of information. *Wired...Red Herring...*Upside...*Teledotcom...*are a few of my favorites. In addition, *The Wall Street Journal, The New York Times* and *Investors Business Daily* each has a section that features articles about the information technology industry.

Whatever industry you might choose as your centerpiece, the value of extensive reading is simply this: The more familiar you become with an industry, the easier it will be for you to identify the areas within that industry that offer the greatest potential for growth. Absent that knowledge or familiarity, it will be difficult for you to identify companies that have a unique competitive advantage–or that have developed products/services for overcoming some of the barriers to growth within their industries. With that familiarity you should be able to discover companies that are near to the beginning of their growth cycle.

Here's an illustration of how reading trade magazines can contribute to the stock selection process. The following was taken from an interview with Howard Janzen, CEO of Williams Communications. Williams is one of several companies that has been building a nationwide fiber optic network.

Q: *Everybody says bandwidth will continue to increase almost infinitely. Why is that?*

A: *I used to get that question a lot from our outside board. You know, with all the capacity that's being built, is the demand going to be enough to consume the capacity? We invited Nathan Myhrvold, the chief technology officer of Microsoft, to speak at a recent board meeting. After his discussion, our board members switched from that mode into the mode of "Are we building enough fiber? Do you have enough conduit? Is this enough?"*

My way of explaining Nathan's message is that today if you look at the way business is conducted, all the agents in the world really represent the sellers. So if you go to buy a car, the agent who's the car salesman does not work for you, he works for General Motors or Ford. He's trying to push the products to you.

With Web technology, that dynamic is changing and the agents are starting to represent the buyers. As that becomes more developed, think of all the computing power that's being deployed. And as computing power continues to grow, that PC can turn into an agent that doesn't need you even sitting at the keyboard. You could launch something to say, "I'm ready to buy a car." Hit one button and that agent already knows what you are looking for, and it searches and finds you the ideal car in the perfect color, the best price, and has it shipped to your door.

The technology is starting to be there. We haven't seen anything yet that reflects the kind of demands for bandwidth when that model starts to take effect.

http://www.teledotcom.com/1098/features/tdc1098inter-view.html

When you acquire that level of information or insight, it ought to provide you with a warm, fuzzy feeling about the potential for future growth within the fiber optics and communications industries. It ought to suggest to you that we are only in the beginning stages of some pretty exciting growth. If you can get a picture in your mind about the longer-term growth potential of an industry, then you can focus on individual companies within that industry with a higher level of confidence. The next step is to find companies within the communications industry that can provide you with the same warm and fuzzy feeling regarding their potential for future growth.

One good way to stay abreast of industry trends–and to discover new portfolio candidates–is to follow the news within your selected industry segment(s). Once again, Yahoo! offers a valuable source that provides daily news updates for specific industries. Return to the main Yahoo!Finance page: http://quote.yahoo.com/.

In the "Financial News" category, click on *By Industry*. You don't have to read every news item. Just scan the headlines. Some phrases are very dynamic and should easily catch your attention. For example, "Record Earnings" or "Breakthrough Technology" suggest that an article is worth reading. This is also a terrific source for learning about some of the key challenges that are facing an industry and the companies that are providing solutions to those problems.

Some of the companies mentioned will be familiar to you. However, you will probably come across some company names that will be totally new to you. Don't simplify the selection process by choosing only the names that are familiar to you. If anyone had eliminated unfamiliar names ten years ago they probably would have missed stocks like Intel, Microsoft and Cisco. One of the intriguing–and challenging, for investors–features of the Information Age is that companies can be created today and become tomorrow's industry leaders within a very short period of time.

In fact, consider the following. Every year International Data Corporation (IDC)–one of the world's largest publishers of technology newspapers and magazines–conducts a nationwide survey of information technology officers. Two of the questions that have been asked are "Which company, today, is the most significant supplier of products/services to your company?" and "Which company, five years from now, will be the most significant supplier of products/services to your company?" In both 1996 and 1997 the leading response to the first question was Microsoft Corp. In both years the overwhelming leading response to the second question was, "That company does not now exist!"

A Somewhat Different–and Shorter–Approach to the Discovery Process

My fantasy portfolio has been able to pretty consistently outperform both the S&P 500 and the NASDAQ Composite from the time it was first launched. However, if you look at the performance chart for that portfolio (see chart at the end of this chapter), you will note that the degree of out-performance has accelerated beginning in the first quarter of 1999. I'm convinced that this acceleration can be attributed to the discovery and subsequent application of the two screening systems that follow. This confirms that the past two and one-half years have been a learning experience for me as well. It also strongly suggests that the systematic learning system prescribed in Chapter 4 does, in fact, work.

By the way, the learning process isn't over for me. The Internet is a work in process. I don't think that anyone can say that they've learned all that there is to learn about investing using the Internet as the principal tool. It seems that every week I discover something new and useful. You will undoubtedly enjoy the same sense of excitement as you discover your own nuggets of information.

There are actually two sources and methodologies that have been responsible for the outstanding performance that began in the first quarter of 1999. Each is very simple to implement, but there are virtues of each that extend far beyond their simplicity. The two sources/methodologies are:

1. *Daily volume analysis*
2. *Quarterly earnings analysis*

Although the two are distinctly different, they share some very positive characteristics. First, however, their differences. The daily volume analysis is mainly reactive in nature, hence the element of discovery is less of a factor than with the quarterly earnings analysis. The earlier one can discover an emerging growth investment opportunity, the higher the potential profits will be. Therefore the daily volume analysis–which is necessarily reactive–is at a slight disadvantage to the quarterly earnings analysis, which is proactive and therefore facilitates early discovery.

That is not to say that the daily volume analysis can't introduce you to some tremendous investment opportunities. It only means that you're not going to be at the very front of the discovery process. Don't let that deter you. You may have to buy a stock that began its run at $10 per share and is now at $15 or $20. If subsequent research suggests to you that the company is headed for extraordinary growth for the foreseeable future, you may have the opportunity to be invested at $15 or $20 with the stock on its way up to $50, $60–or higher!

On the other hand, you can be entirely correct in discovering an emerging growth stock by using the quarterly earnings analysis. It's very possible that you could be at the front of the discovery line. In the previous illustration you could be one of the investors who bought at $10. However, the possibility exists that unless and until other investors make the same discovery, the stock may do nothing for days or months. As you might by now suspect, the daily volume analysis provides an element of timeliness. It reveals that other investors have also discovered this investment opportunity and have voted with their dollars.

The similarities between the two systems are critically important to individual investors. The raw information of each is made available to all investors at the same time. Nobody–absolutely and emphatically nobody–gains a competitive advantage through early access to either source of information. In addition, the information from both sources is empirical. There is no hyperbole. There is no editorializing. There is just raw, unadulterated data.

Let's examine each of the two systems and how you can use them to enhance your investment skills.

1. Screening Quarterly Earnings Reports

All publicly owned companies must file quarterly financial reports with the SEC. These reports are made available to all investors at the same time, nobody gets any sneak previews, thereby gaining an investment edge. The majority of companies use a fiscal year that coincides with the calendar year. In other words, their internal accounting periods coincide with the normal calendar year in that the fiscal year accounting begins on January 1st and ends on December 31st. Therefore, their quarterly financial reports usually cover the three-month periods ending March 31st, June 30th, September 30th and December 31st.

Because it takes time to compile and approve these financial reports, they typically are not available until the 2nd, 3rd or 4th week following the end of each quarter. Consequently, if you focus on the the 2nd, 3rd or 4th weeks of April, July, October and January you will be able to screen a very large number of companies for the financial characteristics that you consider to be important.

However, not all companies have a fiscal year that coincides with the calendar year; you will find that earnings releases occur almost every business day of every month. However, by the time that the third month of each quarter rolls around, the number of companies releasing a quarterly financial report will represent just a trickle.

None of this information is unique to the Internet since all of it–and more–will be available the next day in either *The Wall Street Journal* or

Investor's Business Daily. What is important is that no investor–institutional or individual–will have access to this information sooner than you. The significance of having access to this information on the day that companies release it is simple. If you wait to obtain this information the following day from one of the newspapers, you will necessarily delay doing any follow-up research by one full day.

Keep in mind that the raw material obtained from these sources should not serve as the sole determinant in your stock selection process. Filtering through this data to select companies with minimum performance levels to meet your criteria is a form of quantitative analysis. It serves the purpose of helping you to winnow through the universe of publicly owned companies to find likely candidates for your portfolio.

What minimum performance levels should you be looking for? First of all, I don't pay much attention to earnings or earnings per share. There are three reasons why I don't analyze earnings. The first reason is that most other investors, institutional as well as individual, are almost totally focused on earnings performance. It would be difficult for me to gain a competitive advantage to be similarly focused. The second reason is that companies can readily manipulate earnings when they release their quarterly financial reports. Therefore, my focus is almost entirely on revenues–more specifically, revenue growth. I know that revenues can also be manipulated, but not as easily. Consider the following:

> *Quarterly earnings announcements have been a well-choreographed waltz for some time. As investors relied more on short-term earnings forecasts to help them value shares, astute executives learned to manage expectations for their companies' performance down to a level that they could then breeze past.*
>
> *Evidence of how well companies have managed earnings can be seen in the number of reports that beat Wall Street estimates by a single penny a share. According to Thomson/First Call, of the 311 S&P companies that have reported earnings for the third quarter, 21.5 percent beat their estimates by one cent. In each of the last six*

quarters, 18 percent of companies, on average, beat their estimates by a penny.

Paired with management in the earnings waltz were security analysts who are supposed to conduct independent research on companies they follow. As quarterly earnings numbers became paramount, analysts grew more dependent upon company management for "guidance" to the correct earnings forecast. The more help they received, the less work they did.

This dance went smoothly for awhile. Companies met or beat the analysts' estimates and their stocks went up.

Now, however, many companies who had been great at managing earnings are caught in a vise of rising expectations: A company that merely matches Wall Street's forecasts in a given quarter may see its stock price tank on the news.

http://www.nytimes.com/library/financial/sunday/102499mar-ket-watch.html

Because of these financial shenanigans–from both reporting companies and analysts–I ignore the actual earnings component of the quarterly earnings report. Instead, I look for companies that have increased the current quarter's *revenues* by at least 40% over the same quarter in the previous year.

The third reason is perhaps the most important. The top line of every profit and loss statement is always "Revenues." Unless revenues are increasing there is a distinct limit to how much clever financial management and aggressive cost-cutting campaigns can increase earnings. More important, expanding revenues give a clear indication that a company has products or services that a growing number of consumers are willing to buy. That is unquestionably the best metric available to indicate to investors that a company represents a genuine growth opportunity.

Given the fact that the economy grows, at best, roughly 5% per year, isn't it difficult to find companies that are growing their revenues by

40% or more? I've compiled a database of companies with a quarterly revenue growth rate of 40% or better since the second quarter of 1997. From the second quarter of 1997 through the first quarter of 2000, the average number of companies passing through that screen was roughly 396, with a high of 654 (1st quarter of 2000) and a low of 257 (1st quarter of '99). The average percentage increase in revenues for all companies for that time period was roughly 192%. If you decide to use this method as a screening device, you will have plenty of companies to analyze–particularly in the information technology sector.

There are a couple of ancillary bits of knowledge or conclusions that can be gained from this database. First, it offers an insight about the dynamism of the economy, and therefore of the stock market. Both the number of companies reporting greater than 40% revenue increases, year-over-year, and the average percentage increases have been steadily climbing for this period of time. This tends to support the observation that the underlying economy has been robust. The second observation is that the overwhelming majority of qualifying companies can be categorized as high-tech, with a substantial representation from industries involved with the Internet. This tends to explain the extraordinary market performance of stocks in that industry segment.

Although having access to this information the day it is released may be important in some instances, it has been my experience that the market will frequently offer plenty of time to analyze and respond to these earnings reports. You may miss a point or two, but if you're a long-term investor and you're looking for stocks that have the potential for substantial gains, missing a point or two will not be a detriment. In fact, quite often the price of a stock will decrease after a company has released its quarterly earnings report, even if that report is very positive.

Why? A lot of investors acquire a stock in anticipation of a good earnings report being announced by the company. Once the good news has been announced, these investors sell their stock since the anticipation of good news no longer exists. The announcement itself is almost anticlimactic. This phenomenon seems to be particularly true when the overall market sentiment is bullish.

There are a couple of other reasons why stocks don't always move sharply higher in response to good earnings reports. One of the most obvious reasons is that analysts need time to review the financial statements that usually accompany an earnings release. This is particularly true if the issuing company is relatively unknown and doesn't have any or many analysts following the stock. If the earnings report is the first exposure that an analyst has to that company, he/she will have to spend some time doing further research before offering a buy recommendation.

A second reason illustrates one of the advantages that individual investors have over institutional investors. If an institutional investor–the manager of a mutual fund, for example–genuinely likes the longer-term potential for an individual stock, he/she will want to acquire a substantial position in that stock. It's not unusual for most mutual fund managers to purchase a million or more shares of a specific stock. If these institutional investors attempted to buy the number of shares that they eventually want to own in one or two days, the price would move sharply higher, thereby increasing their cost basis. Rather than do that, the fund managers pace their purchases over an extended period of time. Also, bear in mind that if one fund manager finds a particular stock attractive, the chances are pretty good that other fund managers will also want to acquire that stock.

In contrast, you as an individual investor can jump right into the market with your smaller purchase. You can then sit back and enjoy the steady increase in the market value of your newly acquired stock as the institutional investors gradually accumulate the number of shares they have programmed for purchase over the following days, weeks and months. Naturally all of this assumes that you are looking for and have identified stocks with the same financial characteristics that the institutions are looking for.

Of course, there's a flip side to this advantage. As an individual investor, you normally will have no difficulties liquidating your position when you decide to move out of a stock. Institutional investors don't have that luxury. Because of the large number of shares that they typically own, they have to parcel out their sales over an extended period of time. If they opted to sell their entire position in one day, the result would probably be a precipitous decline in the market value of that stock.

There is an additional advantage that you might experience. If, for example, you're looking for companies with consistent and extraordinary revenue growth, the chances are pretty good that one of the financial newspapers or magazines will also detect those companies. They know that if they can discover and write a report on emerging growth companies, doing so will help them to sell their magazines or newspapers. It will take those publications some time to collect their information, write their stories and eventually publish. When the story finally appears–assuming that it's presented with a positive bias–a new wave of buying will occur from all of those investors who read the newspaper or magazine article.

But, getting back to our quarterly earnings report analysis, the most user-friendly source for this information that I've been able to find is *Investor's Business Daily* (IBD). In fact, every day during the four earnings-reporting seasons there is a chart in IBD that ranks the companies with the largest percentage increase in earnings. This list also details the percentage increase in revenue, the profit margin and the level of revenues for each company. The problem that I have with this convenient chart is that the ranking is based on the percentage increase in earnings, whereas my recommendation is that you focus on trying to identify companies with the greatest increase in revenues.

Consequently, in order to perform the screening for revenue growth effectively it's necessary to look at every company report that is listed every day. Even with this careful scrutiny, IBD offers a significant advantage over *The Wall Street Journal* in that they compute the percentage increase in revenues and the profit margin for every company whose earnings report is listed. (There is an exception to this–the percentage increase of revenues for banks and certain other financial institutions is not reported.) Hence, you will be able to easily scan every day's listings for the percentage increase in revenues for each company because that percentage increase is in bold type. In contrast, *The Wall Street Journal* simply lists the data without this vital information about percentage increases.

There is an alternative to this daily ritual. If you want to develop your own financial parameters for selecting stocks and don't want to get involved with the daily ritual of screening earnings reports, one of the best sources for doing this is http://hoovers.com/search/forms/stockscreener/. This site will enable you to enter financial screens that you consider being important. For example, you can scan the universe of stocks for companies that have grown revenues by at least 50%, that have a profit margin of at least 20% and that have a P/E ratio of less than 30. Entering those limits will produce a list of stocks that have those financial characteristics. Since this database is continuously updated–although not in a timely manner–it can be used at any time of the year. You don't have to wait for the "earnings-reporting seasons" mentioned earlier.

For those of you who want to gain access to a daily summary of companies releasing quarterly earnings that includes revenue growth rates, the best source that I've been able to find is located here: http://www.briefing.com/sub/stocks/earncal.htm.

You'll have to subscribe to this site, but the price is nominal–roughly $9.00 per month. I haven't analyzed the comprehensiveness or the accuracy of the information provided. However, I have been able to corroborate the accuracy of this information for most of the companies that I've picked out for further research. I use this source almost daily, since it provides me with a simple listing of companies reporting for each day and–most important–the percentage increase in reported revenues for the current quarter vis-à-vis the year ago quarter. It has also been the source for the database of quarterly revenue growth that was mentioned earlier in this chapter.

There's another good source for spotting companies with extraordinary revenue and earnings growth rates–and it's free. At the end of every week *The Motley Fool* publishes a list of companies that have reported earnings during the previous week. This report shows the percentage increase in revenues and earnings. However, the unique and valuable feature of this list is that it identifies just those companies that have earnings and revenue gains of at least 15%…and expanding profit margins. The latter statistic reflects effective management and/or lack of competitive pricing pressures. The web site for this information is:

http://www.fool.com/Stockscreens/risingmargins.htm

2. Screening Daily Activity Reports

This is a nifty screen. As the saying goes, "This is where the rubber meets the road!" To illustrate the effectiveness of this screen, answer this question: If you wanted to buy a stock based on the advice of someone who is respected and knowledgeable, would you buy the stock they said you should buy, or the one that they bought for themselves? Individual and institutional investors can extol the virtues of a particular stock at cocktail parties and other public forums ad infinitum. Stories can be "planted" in various financial publications trumpeting those same virtues. None of that should influence your thinking, although most of the time that is precisely the intent of the talk and the articles.

The only thing that matters is when investors, individual or institutional, actually spend their money to buy the stock. Fortunately, the number of shares traded in every stock on any given day on any of the exchanges or in the over-the-counter market is made available to the public after the close of business every day. Once again, nobody obtains an investment advantage by gaining early access to this information. And, there is no PR fluff–it's all empirical data. If institutional investors, with their superior sources of information, truly believe a company's stock will increase in market value, they won't talk about it–they will buy it. And those purchases, if they represent a significant commitment on the part of the institutions, will almost always be reflected in an increase in the volume of shares traded for that company. Similarly, since information travels so quickly among communities of individual investors on the Internet, the news of an investment discovery will often result in a surge of buying which will create an extraordinary increase in the number of shares traded.

These surges in activity are precisely what you should be looking for. For example, if a stock normally has 100,000 shares traded on an average day, you wouldn't get too excited if one day it had 125,000 shares traded. However, if you notice that one day there were 5,000,000 shares of that stock traded, that should pique your curiosity. That spike in activity should tell you that something unusual and exciting is happening with that company. More important, it should tell you that a lot of investors, or a few investors with a lot of money, have learned about that unusual and exciting event. All hype aside, these investors are also showing that they are willing to put their money where their mouth is.

There are two sources that I use for identifying extraordinary volume. The first source can be found at http://equities.barchart.com/. As you explore the information available on this page you will undoubtedly develop your own preferences in terms of what information is the most useful. Let me get you started by mentioning my preferences and the reasons that I find them useful.

52 Week Highs.

If you look at any proven growth-company chart, one reality is indisputable: It has steadily made new 52-week highs. You should be cautioned that a new high doesn't guarantee that the stock will continue climbing. All it suggests is that something is happening within the company to cause investors to view the future with increasing optimism. Your challenge is to make a determination as to whether that optimism is justified and whether or not it is likely to continue in the future. Remember, if a stock is destined to go from 25 to 50 and it's currently at 30, it necessarily has to hit a lot of new highs along the way. It's unfortunate, but some investors view new highs with a different perspective. They think that it's too late to invest in stocks trading at new highs. They prefer to invest in stocks trading at new lows, believing that those stocks are like merchandise in Filene's basement–great values at discounted prices. I believe that it's easier to determine the likelihood that stocks hitting new highs will continue on that path than it is to determine the likelihood that stocks trading at new lows will reverse their trend.

Volume Leaders.

This metric gives investors an excellent picture relative to where the preponderance of investment money is going. You shouldn't get too excited about some of the big names that appear regularly on this list. However, an irregular appearance should pique your interest. Let me explain. Big stocks, like Microsoft, Intel, IBM, etc., will almost always appear as volume leaders. However, if one day you spot an unfamiliar stock on the Volume Leader list, that would warrant further investigation. One other point: Unless you're interested in identifying stocks that you might want to sell short, disregard stocks that appear on the Volume Leader list and that have declined in market value. In fact, if you own a stock that appears on this list and it has declined in value, that might be a signal for you to get rid of that stock.

% Increases.

This category lists the stocks that have had the largest percent increase in market value. There are two caveats that should be mentioned. First, if a stock is not actively traded or if there are just a couple of companies that make a market in the stock, a modest increase in volume might result in an inordinate increase in price. Consequently I try to focus on those companies on this list that have had at least 500,000 shares traded.

Second, when a stock rises precipitously–particularly if it's a low priced stock–it attracts short-sellers as rapidly as blood attracts sharks!

(See discussion of short-selling at end of this chapter.) Their thinking is that once the euphoria of good news has been disseminated throughout the investment community, buying activity will abate since there will be no further motivation to buy. Therefore, normal selling will result in the price of that stock declining towards its previous level. Having dispensed with these caveats, I can mention that the % Increase category has been, for me, the best source of investment ideas on the barchart.com page.

The second source for extraordinary volume is also my favorite source. It can be found at http://www.bigcharts.com/reports/. The most significant disadvantage of this page vis-à-vis barchart.com is that it has been available only on the following morning, whereas much of the information on barchart.com is updated throughout the day, making it more current than bigcharts.com. The category that I use almost exclusively on bigcharts.com is "Stocks with the largest % gain in volume" on the NASDAQ. To quote directly from that site:

> This report ranks the top stocks with a closing price of 12 or higher, a price change of a half point or greater, and a 50-day average volume of 25,000 based on their percentage increase in daily trading volume. On a daily basis BigCharts compares each stock's percentage volume change relative to the stock's average trading volume over the past 50 trading days.

I've been unable to find any other source on the Internet that matches the comprehensiveness and the utility of the information on this site. What every investor should be interested in is a significant increase in the volume of shares traded. The message delivered by this information is that a discovery is in process. Some positive development is occurring within that company and investors have discovered that development. Whatever the reason, the investor supply/demand curves have shifted decidedly in favor of demand and in the final analysis, that's what causes market values to increase. The number of investors wanting to buy increases while the number of owners of the stock wanting to sell decreases.

More than once I've quietly chided myself for not taking action on stocks that have appeared on this list and subsequently soared in value. If I were given the choice of one–and only one–site on the Internet that could be used for selecting stocks, this would be it.

Is That All There Is to the Discovery Process?

In a word–"No." In fact, it's just the beginning. Both the quarterly earnings analysis and the daily volume analysis are retrospective in nature. They present historical data. On their own, they have no predictive value. Unfortunately, successful investing requires an ability to predict–or more accurately, make an educated guess about–future market performance. I'm not aware of any tools or any sources on the Internet that can help to make this more of a science and less of an art. However, there are tools and sources that can increase the likelihood that your investment decisions will be significantly better than *not* using these tools and these sources.

Here again, you will develop your own methods and your own sources for collecting more information about companies that have been filtered through your initial screens. However, as an aid to kick-start your efforts, let me take you through a step-by-step discussion of the sources used in my stock selection process.

Let's begin by assuming that we've identified an interesting company using either the quarterly earnings analysis or the unusual activity analysis. A company I picked purely at random and only for purposes of illustrating the process is *Advanced Energy Industries* (AEIS-NASDAQ).

http://quote.yahoo.com/. This is where it all begins. In the blank to the left of "Get Quotes," type the stock symbol AEIS. To the right of "Get Quotes" is a pull-down menu. Select "Detailed" and hit Enter. The ensuing page gives you a good historical picture of AEIS, including the Last Trade, the 52-week Range and a small one-year price performance chart. At the bottom of the page can be found "Recent News" items.

Look for the most recent Quarterly Earnings Announcement. This provides a glimpse of what the revenue growth has been and also gives management the opportunity to comment on the factors contributing to that growth. Other Recent News headlines should be scanned for releases that might shed some light on future developments.

If the nature of the company's business is not clear from reading the Quarterly Earnings Announcement, click on "Profile" which is located just above the chart. At the bottom of the Profile page is a "Business Summary" which offers a concise explanation of what the company does. If you still don't know the exact nature of the company's business, click on "Home Page," which is located just below "Company's Web Presence." When you get to the Home Page, go to the "Investor Relations" section. It will contain a plethora of information that is useful to all investors and will almost certainly provide you with an understanding of the company's business. It's important to know what products or services are offered by the company so that you can make a judgment relative to whether or not the company can continue on a growth path.

At the top of the Profile page is a line entitled "More Info." The references that follow that title contain some of the most useful pages of information that can be found on the Internet. Let's look in more detail at three of those referenced pages.

Research.

The upper-left box will inform you of the number of analysts who follow the stock along with their investment rating. Although it may be comforting to observe that most of the analysts covering the stock have a "Strong Buy" or "Buy" rating, you probably shouldn't accord too much weight to those ratings. The most important information on this page is contained in the upper-right box: "Consensus Estimates" for future earnings per share. Since in the final analysis all stock market values are ultimately tied to earnings per share, the importance of this information can't be overstated. Furthermore, since these estimates are pretty much spoon-fed to the analysts by the CFO or the CEO of the respective companies, there is an element of credibility. In any event, these numbers represent the best opportunity for investors to attempt to establish a future market value for the stock under consideration.

This is important enough to warrant an illustration. At the time of this analysis, AEIS was selling at $38. Stocks usually sell at a multiple of projected earnings per share. The consensus estimate for AEIS's earnings-per-share in FY 2000 (ending in December) was $1.23. By deduction, AEIS was then trading at roughly 30 times next year's earnings. That PE ratio wasn't much higher than the PE ratio of the overall market. However, in order to determine whether or not that represents good value, an assessment has to be made about the prospects for continued future growth. AEIS's earnings per share were projected to grow over 175% in 2000 versus 1999. More important, the revenue for the last quarter increased 95% over the year-ago quarter. If those rates of revenue growth and earnings-per-share growth could be extended beyond 2000, then the stock was definitely a bargain. That last sentence began with an important word: "If." The challenge for all investors is to acquire as much information as possible that might enable them to convert "if" to "when."

Another valuable source of information, "Earnings Growth," can be found by scrolling down the page. This section provides excellent benchmarks for comparative analysis, not only to the overall market but also to a composite of other companies within the industry. The latter is particularly important since, all other things being equal, companies within the same industry should have similar market valuations. In the instance of AEIS, you will note that its earnings were projected to grow slightly faster than the industry composite over the next five years, but–of greater significance–both the industry and AEIS were projected to grow at almost four times the rate of growth of companies in the S&P 500. Therefore, deductive reasoning suggests that if the S&P 500 index can justify a price-to-earnings ratio of 26.3, then AEIS was clearly reasonably priced–perhaps even under-valued–with a price-to-earnings ratio (next year's) of 30.

SEC.

You, as an investor, will never obtain more pertinent information about a company than what can be found in reports submitted by the company to the Securities & Exchange Commission. Clicking on "SEC" will bring you to a condensed version of SEC filings. You can go to http://freeedgar.com/ to get the full text of all of the company's recent filings. You won't find any future projections in the SEC filings, but it's highly likely that you'll find some valuable bits of information not found in any other source. It's dry, repetitive reading, but potentially very rewarding.

Messages

I believe that no source of information on the Internet–or anywhere else–has as much potential as the "Messages" board. The important word in that sentence is "potential." We're not there yet. At the core of my optimism is the following quote:

> *Imagine a meeting where all attendees bring one tangible object and one idea. The objects and ideas are shared. Everyone leaves with only one object, but each departs with as many ideas as there are attendees. What results from the meeting is distinctly different from what was brought to the meeting. Whenever ideas are shared, the result is always greater than the sum of the parts.*
> http://www.FORBES.com/assap/1202961/html/RICH_WILLIS.htm

There's a powerful force that leads me to believe that "Messages" will become the most important source of investment information on the Internet. Let's assume that you discover a company in your city/town that is publicly owned and growing dramatically. Obviously the first thing you or any investor will do is make an investment in that company. It's axiomatic that we all make investments with the anticipation–hope?–that the value of that investment will grow. Once the investment has been made in the company we've discovered, we typically wait for others to make the same discovery. With the advent of the Internet and message boards, we can shorten the time that it takes for other investors to discover "our" stock by disclosing our discovery to them.

The discovery doesn't have to be a company in your own back yard. For example, if you're a research chemist and become aware of a company that has developed some leading edge technology that has the potential to dramatically expand that company's earnings and revenues, you will naturally want to make an investment in that company. Once your investment has been made, there is absolutely no reason why you wouldn't want to share your discovery with other investors. Let me say that differently, there is every reason in the world why you would want to share that discovery! By increasing the number of people who discover the investment merits of this company you will be increasing the number of potential investors (demand) and decreasing the number of current owners of the stock who are willing to sell (supply). Combining those two forces will invariably lead to higher stock prices, which is what every investor wants.

Here, again, some caveats are necessary. This source has the potential for abuses perpetrated by conniving individuals who present inaccurate or misleading information. For that reason, I believe that at some time in the future it ought to be mandatory that every publicly owned company must designate an employee(s) whose primary responsibility is to monitor message boards to be sure that any information posted there is accurate. I also believe that the SEC ought to have a heightened responsibility to monitor message boards and to impose penalties on individuals who deliberately post inaccurate or misleading information. Unless and until these safeguards are in place, most of the information found on message boards should be viewed with caution.

When preparing this book I came across a wonderful quote that is particularly relevant to message boards:

We can learn much from wise words, little from wise cracks
and less from wise guys.
William Arthur Ward

The present state of message boards is that there is much that can be characterized as "wise cracks" from "wise guys." Message boards need more participation from individuals offering "wise words." If sponsors of message boards would prevent anyone from posting unless they revealed their true identify–rather than pseudonyms–the wise cracks and wise guys might disappear.

The information that is posted on message boards doesn't have to be positive in order for it to have value for investors. All investors should welcome negative as well as positive news. Just as early discovery of positive news can enhance your profits when buying a stock, early discovery of negative news will help you to sell that stock before the bottom drops out!

Since investing is preponderantly an activity of positive expectations, you might wonder why anyone would post negative information about a stock on a message board. My experience has been that there is a very healthy dose of negative postings. Most of those messages come from people who have sold the stock short, and posting negative news is a method they use to persuade owners of the stock to sell or to dissuade potential buyers from buying. If they are successful in motivating enough selling–while discouraging others from investing–the resulting lower demand and higher supply will invariably drive the price of the stock down and the short sellers can make money.

Just a few words about short-selling. Most investors are aware that the way to make money is to buy low and at some point in the future sell high. Short-sellers believe that they can make money by reversing that process by first selling high and then buying low. That begs the question: How can they sell something that they don't own? The answer is that they borrow the stock from brokerage firms. When you open a margin account with a brokerage firm you probably signed a margin agreement which, among other things, gave the brokerage firm the right to loan your stocks to anyone who might want to sell those stocks short.

Short-selling is inordinately risky. When you buy a stock, you know exactly how much money you can potentially lose–the amount of your investment. On the other hand, the amount of potential profit that you might make is unlimited. When you sell a stock short, the reverse is true. You know exactly the amount of your potential profit. If you sell a stock short at $20, the limit to the amount of money you can make is $20 . To illustrate, if the short-seller is right, the stock could decline to just pennies, at which point the short-seller would buy it and return it to the brokerage firm. The profit would have been close to $20 per share. But, the amount of money that can potentially be lost is *unlimited*. Every $1 increase in the market value of that stock above $20 represents a dollar of potential loss for the short-seller. In addition, short-selling is like buying on margin in that there are minimum margin requirements. For example, if the stock shorted at $20 goes to $30, the short-seller would either have to buy the stock back at a loss or deposit more money into his/her account.

One of the ditties that every stockbroker learns early in his/her career is the following:

He who borrows what isn't his'n, must buy it back or go to prison!

In view of the severity of the losses that can be incurred if they're wrong, short-sellers tend to do their homework more thoroughly than most investors. Therefore, their input on message boards can be very valuable. However, once again there has to be a tremendous temptation for them to be overly dramatic and perhaps even to stretch the truth a bit in their efforts to convince buyers or potential buyers that the price of the stock is about to drop in value.

Maintenance Program

Perhaps the following should have been mentioned in the beginning of this chapter. If you're a comparative beginner to the world of investing and are befuddled by some of the investment terminology that you've encountered, I recommend that you go to http://www.fool.com/school/13steps/13steps.htm and read the "Thirteen Steps to Investing Foolishly." This contains some wonderful stuff, is easy reading and will bring you up to speed quickly.

Once you've arrived at the point where you feel very comfortable about making investment decisions using the methods presented in this book, it's a good idea to resist the temptation to put the process on "automatic pilot" with no further efforts on your part. Investing is like any other pursuit in that success isn't a destination–it's a continuing process. Today, it's a rare stock indeed that you can buy and put in your safe deposit box for 10 or 20 years.

The amount of time that will be required for maintaining your investment skills will have to be determined by you. But make no mistake about it–you will have to commit a certain amount of time each week, if not every day, to the process of continuing your learning. You won't have to commit as much time to the maintenance process as you did to the basic learning with your fantasy portfolio. The nature of this discovery process ought to represent a welcome challenge, perhaps even a source of enjoyment for you. If you fail to capture and rise to that sense of challenge, or if you fail to experience enjoyment from the discovery process, then perhaps you ought to seek out a professional investment advisor who can perform the maintenance function for you.

What's involved in the maintenance program? I would encourage you to continue using the two discovery methods outlined in this chapter. Since your stock selection skills have been honed, resulting in a higher quality of stocks in your "real world" portfolio, it's not going to be necessary to go through the discovery process as frequently as you did while learning with the fantasy portfolio. However, by now you should have acquired an understanding of how vital it is to remain aware of what's happening in the economy and within your chosen industry segment(s). Simply put, your pursuit of profitable investments will be somewhat crippled if you totally discontinue the learning process.

If you haven't learned it thus far, you will undoubtedly learn soon that with today's rapidly changing economic environment, monitoring your investments is almost as important as making the initial selections. The following is a brief compilation of the basic elements of my maintenance program. I devote anywhere from a half-hour to a full hour every day to this program.

Business
http://interactive.wsj.com/pages/front.htm
http://www.nytimes.com/yr/mo/day/business/
http://www.investors.com/web_edition/today/welcome.html
http://www.mercurycenter.com/business/
http://cbs.marketwatch.com/news/newsroom.htx

Technology
http://interactive.wsj.com/pages/techmain.htm#top
http://news.com/
http://www.redherring.com/insider/home.html
http://www.wired.com/news/technology/
http://www.upside.com/
http://www.teledotcom.com/

Of those sources, the only one that you will have to pay for is *The Wall Street Journal*, but the annual cost–about $52–is a bargain considering the rich content and the ease of use versus the newspaper itself.

If your appetite for information can't be met by these sources, you might want to go to http://www.ceoexpress.com/ and select your own sources.

Date	Portfolio	% Change	S&P 500	% Change	Nasdaq	% Change
Apr-97	$250,000	0.00%	765.37	0.00%	1209.29	0.00%
May-97	$356,947	42.78%	848.28	10.83%	1400.32	15.80%
Jun-97	$349,710	39.88%	887.30	15.93%	1438.15	18.93%
Jul-97	$395,136	58.05%	938.79	22.66%	1569.58	29.79%
Aug-97	$428,334	71.33%	899.47	17.52%	1587.32	31.26%
Sep-97	$416,672	66.67%	945.22	23.50%	1682.24	39.11%
Oct-97	$356,916	42.77%	914.62	19.50%	1593.61	31.78%
Nov-97	$320,750	28.30%	955.40	24.83%	1600.55	32.35%
Dec-97	$283,750	13.50%	936.46	22.35%	1511.38	24.98%
Jan-98	$323,502	29.40%	980.28	28.08%	1619.36	33.91%
Feb-98	$378,222	51.29%	1049.34	37.10%	1770.51	46.41%
Mar-98	$417,116	66.85%	1095.44	43.13%	1823.62	50.80%
Apr-98	$504,639	101.86%	1107.90	44.75%	1868.96	54.55%
May-98	$514,017	105.61%	1090.82	42.52%	1778.87	47.10%
Jun-98	$577,896	131.16%	1133.20	48.06%	1869.53	54.60%
Jul-98	$571,295	128.52%	1120.67	46.42%	1872.39	54.83%
Aug-98	$423,708	69.48%	1027.14	34.20%	1639.68	35.59%
Sep-98	$460,485	84.19%	1044.75	36.50%	1743.59	44.18%
Oct-98	$484,051	93.62%	1098.67	43.55%	1771.39	46.48%
Nov-98	$607,625	143.05%	1192.33	55.78%	2016.44	66.75%
Dec-98	$655,702	162.28%	1229.23	60.61%	2192.69	81.32%
Jan-99	$737,668	195.07%	1279.64	67.19%	2505.89	107.22%
Feb-99	$685,887	174.35%	1238.33	61.79%	2288.03	89.20%
Mar-99	$784,789	213.92%	1282.80	67.61%	2419.17	100.05%
Apr-99	$1,074,660	329.86%	1335.18	74.45%	2542.86	110.28%
May-99	$1,236,515	394.61%	1301.84	70.09%	2470.52	104.30%
Jun-99	$1,352,512	441.00%	1315.31	71.85%	2793.07	130.97%
Jul-99	$1,511,153	504.46%	1328.72	73.60%	2638.49	118.19%
Aug-99	$1,832,570	633.03%	1348.27	76.16%	2758.89	128.14%
Sep-99	$1,986,078	694.43%	1277.36	66.89%	2740.41	126.61%
Oct-99	$2,792,792	1017.12%	1362.93	78.07%	3102.29	156.54%
Nov-99	$4,096,905	1538.76%	1416.61	85.09%	3447.81	185.11%
Dec-99	$5,516,945	2106.78%	1469.25	91.97%	4069.31	236.50%
Jan-00	$7,021,526	2708.61%	1394.46	82.19%	3887.07	221.43%
Feb-00	$11,162,585	4365.03%	1366.42	78.53%	4590.5	279.60%
Mar-00	$7,687,670	2975.07%	1498.58	95.80%	3321.29	174.65%
Apr-00	$9,534,698	3713.88%	1448.15	89.21%	3860.66	219.25%

Three-year history of personal fantasy portfolio.

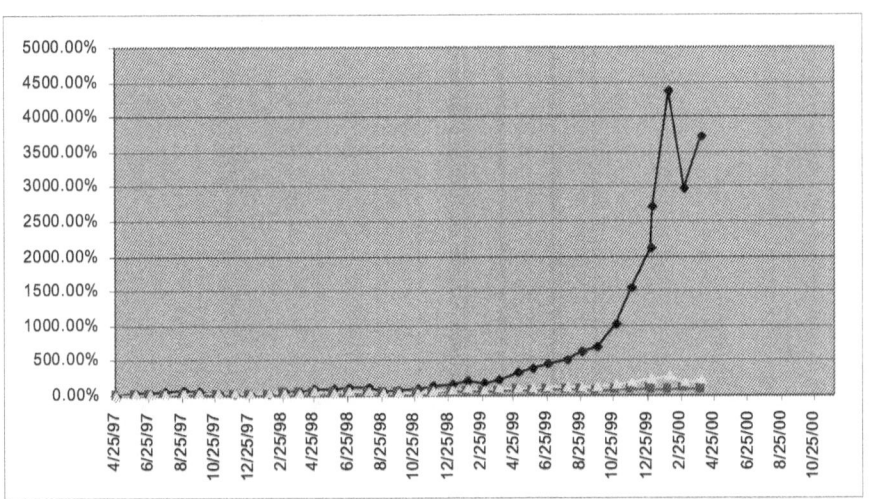

Chapter 4

Opportunities for All Investors

"Imagine a meeting where all attendees bring one tangible object and one idea. The objects and ideas are shared. Everyone leaves with only one object, but each departs with as many ideas as there are attendees. What results from the meeting is distinctly different from what was brought to the meeting. Whenever ideas are shared, the result is always greater than the sum of the parts."

http://www.FORBES.com/assap/1202961/html/RICH_WILLIS.htm

After the Learning…What Then?

The above quote offers a succinct explanation of the essential value of the Internet. It is precisely the sharing of ideas, and the ubiquity of access to the thoughts and ideas of other people, that gives the Internet its awesome potential. There are two ways for you to embark into the world of investing with real money.

You can do it on your own…just you and the Internet.

You can do it in concert with a select group of other individuals, all committed to the discovery of emerging growth stock investment opportunities using the Internet as the principle search vehicle.

A couple of points might be useful before you begin. First of all, it's not necessary that you have $250,000 to begin building your real money portfolio. I'm not sure what the minimum amount of money should be for starting this program. The reason that you should be concerned about a minimum dollar amount to begin your portfolio is that commissions erode your nest egg every time a trade is made. If you're entering your trades with an online brokerage firm, those commission expenses won't be very significant. If you're entering your trades with a full-service brokerage firm, they will be significant and very erosive. Just bear in mind that commission expenses, as expressed as a percentage of your overall investment assets, will increase as the size of your investment assets decreases. If pressed, I would suggest that $25,000 might be the minimum amount of money that anyone should dedicate to creating a real money portfolio, on your own, using the guidelines presented in this book.

The second point that I want to make is that it's not necessary for you to terminate existing relationships that you might have with full-service brokers. In fact, what you have learned thus far will enhance that relationship since your expectations from your broker will be at a higher level. You will have a clearer idea of what information you should expect from him or her in order to enhance your discovery processes. In addition, your clearer investment focus–if adequately communicated to your broker–should help him or her to provide you with supplemental information from his or her research department. In short, the information flow between you and your broker should become bi-directional, rather than the typical uni-directional flow from broker to client.

However, you should certainly make an effort to quantify or measure the value of recommendations and supplemental information forth-coming from your broker. If it becomes clear that there is no value added by the flow of information from your broker to the performance of your portfolio then it would be wise for you to terminate that rela-tionship. You should then either seek out another broker or just execute your trades with an online brokerage firm.

This concept of expanding your sources of information can even be applied to an activity that has become the bane of every investor...unsolicited cold calls from brokers seeking to establish a business relationship. Any broker aspiring to expand his/her business has to make these calls. Be assured that most brokers would love to find an alternative to making cold calls. Sometimes they even can be amus-ingly creative, as witnessed by the following anecdote.

When I was going through brokerage training in 1966, we were told the story of a commodity broker who was trying to build his business. He would call 100 people every day. When talking to the first 50 people he would recommend that they sell a specific commodity. When talking to the second 50, he would recommend that they buy the same com-modity. Commodity markets being what they are, he was quite sure that within a short period of time–usually a few days or perhaps a week or two–the market for that commodity would go either up or down. If the market went up after his original call, there were 50 people who received his buy recommendation. If the market went down after his original call, there were 50 people who received his sell recommendation.

Whether the market value for that commodity went up or down, the broker would now have 50 people who had received a profitable recommendation. That same routine would be repeated; that is, the first 25 people called would receive a buy recommendation for another commodity and the next 25 would receive a sell recommendation for that same commodity. Once again, if the market moved up, he would call the people given the buy recommendation. If it moved down, he would call the people given the sell recommendation. By the time the third call was made to the remaining 25 prospects, most had become believers in his ability to forecast moves in the commodities markets. They were usually quite willing to finally become clients.

Putting creative humor aside, there is a way to convert those persistent cold calls from stockbrokers into a constructive, mutually respectful experience, one that offers the potential to broaden your sources of information. Here's how that can be done.

I once had a customer who would always listen to investment ideas that were offered by brokers making cold calls. He wouldn't respond to the first such call, but would encourage the broker to continue calling with other ideas. He recorded all of the recommendations that he received and monitored their subsequent price action. If a broker consistently presented ideas that were carefully researched and that subsequently increased in value, my client would agree to do business with that broker.

That philosophy struck me as being very sensible. Contrast that with folks who peremptorily hang up when receiving a call from an unknown stockbroker. Rather than being annoyed by the intrusiveness of the unwanted call, wouldn't it be more productive if these folks would simply say something like the following:

I appreciate your calling me. However, I have an unwavering philosophy that I never do business with anyone on the first call. If you have an investment idea that you want to share with me, let me hear it. In addition, I encourage you to call me in the future with

other investment ideas that you might have. After a period of time,
I will make a decision as to whether or not I will open an account
with your firm. That decision will be predicated upon my analysis
of the recommendations that you have made to me.

A communication like that is close to a "win-win" situation. First of
all, it removes the negative and adversarial nature of most broker cold
calls. Secondly, it has the potential to provide you with a new flow of
investment information. However, most important, you can rest
assured that most brokers will think very carefully before calling you
again. You will have placed them on notice that their recommendations
are being monitored.

My experience as a broker with this type of situation was that I never
called back unless and until I had one of those "can't miss" investment
recommendations. If you adopt this type of attitude towards those
unwanted cold calls, you could very well open the door to an expanded
universe of investment discoveries.

An Alternative for the Average Investor–Investment Clubs

Even if you have $250,000 or more available for investing, you might
not want to disrupt your current investment programs by committing
$250,000 to the programs espoused in this book. If that's the case, you
may question how you can repeat in the real world what you accom-
plished with your fantasy portfolio.

The answer to that question is that it's not necessary to have
$250,000 available for investing in order to gain some benefit from the
investment ideas offered in this book. In order to discover what those
alternatives might be, one need only look at where most individuals
with smaller amounts of money currently invest. According to the
National Association of Investors Corp. in Madison Heights, Michigan,
there are currently almost 40,000 investment clubs in the U.S. today,
which is almost double the number of clubs that existed in 1995.

As a preamble to this discussion it's important to recognize that there
are basically two types of investors, passive and active. Passive investors

don't want to be bothered with making investment decisions. Those with limited funds typically send their money off to a mutual fund. Those with more substantial investment assets typically send their money to an investment management firm. In either case, they rely on the skills of professional investors to make all of their investment decisions and are content to receive a quarterly report showing the performance of their investment.

Active investors want to have control over their investment decisions. It's very difficult for active investors with limited funds to construct a diversified portfolio of 15 stocks. Whereas passive investors have literally thousands of mutual funds and investment advisors to choose from, active investors with limited investment assets basically have just one alternative to facilitate the diversification of their investments. That alternative is an investment club.

I've had some experience with investment clubs, both as a participant and as a broker advising investment clubs. Conceptually, investment clubs are an ideal investment alternative for most investors. However, most investment clubs have inherent flaws in their fundamental structures, including the following:

1. The amount of money that most clubs have available for investing, particularly in the beginning, is too small.
2. Most investment clubs are far too conservative in their investment decisions.
3. The decision making process is too slow.

Let's analyze each of these shortcomings more carefully and explore alternatives to each.

Amount of money is too small.

Many of the individuals who participated in the investment clubs that I worked with did so with just a small portion of the overall amount of money they had available for investing. This always struck me as being a paradox. Why? Because there are basically two abiding virtues of an investment club:

1. The pooling of funds offers the potential for better diversification, therefore lower risk, than what each of the individual members could achieve on their own.
2. The opening quote for this chapter captures the virtue of sharing thoughts. If all members embrace a common investment philosophy, the results of many minds devoted to the discovery process will almost inevitably lead to better investment performance.

By the way, those two objectives–better returns and lower risk–are the ultimate objectives of every investor, whether they are professional or amateur, individual or institutional. The truly exciting thing about investment clubs is that they offer perhaps the penultimate opportunity to maximize each of those objectives.

I've broached the idea of having investors commit more of their assets to the investment club concept with a few of my stockbroker friends. Their responses to this thought have all been the same: Individual investors will not want to commit more than a token percentage of their overall investment assets to investment clubs. The reason offered for this conclusion is that individual investors will not want to have a significant portion of their investment wealth controlled by the decisions of a group.

If you look again at the quintessential values of belonging to an investment club–to wit, lower risk through diversification and higher returns through the collective thinking of many minds–the argument against committing a higher percentage of one's investment funds to the club concept is flawed. The key to achieving those two values, however, is that all members must have the same investment objectives. The concepts presented in this book, if embraced by all club members, has the potential to create the necessary uniformity of investment objectives.

If I am wrong about this premise and my stockbroker friends are right, then most investment clubs will almost always have an insufficient amount of money available for investing, particularly when launched. Let me try to illustrate that point.

Most investment clubs will launch with anywhere from 10 to 20 members. Typically each new member will be asked for an initial investment of anywhere from $500 to $1,000. Monthly contributions are usually in the $25 to $50 range.

Let's make some assumptions and follow through with the mathematical projections. Let's assume that a club gets started with 15 members, each contributing an initial $1,000 and subsequent monthly contributions of $50. Finally, let's assume that the club can achieve a 10% compound annual growth rate on their investments.

At the end of the first year, this club will have an investment portfolio valued at a bit more than $25,000, which I would consider a minimum amount for anyone opting to create their own portfolio. Consequently, the entire first year of the club's existence will have been spent creating a bare minimum level of investment funds for an individual portfolio! If they choose to distribute that amount of money among the stocks of 15 companies, the club will be able to purchase about 50 shares of stock for each company.

However, the important point that I want to make is that–using the assumptions of the preceding chapters–the club will not have $250,000 in available funds until the end of the *twelfth* year. There's nothing magical about that $250,000 amount. This club can still provide the members with a good education with the scheduled level of investments. But, if in fact the 10% compound annual growth is attainable–and history proves that it is–then why not explore the possibility of increasing the investment commitments to the club right from the beginning? In fact, there is reason to believe that the inherent potential for lower risk and higher return of investment clubs might generate returns higher than the 10% compound annual growth rate.

Wouldn't the members of the club be provided with a far more stimulating and educational experience if the membership was expanded to 25 and each member was required to contribute $10,000 when the club was created? Although monthly contributions could continue if desired, the suggested $50 amount would be relatively insignificant and could probably be eliminated. In fact, if the performance of the club succeeds in beating the performance of the overall market, members might want to make more substantial incremental contributions to the club.

It's probably not a good idea for any club to launch their actual investing program with $250,000 without doing some preparatory work. I would suggest that the club follow the recommendations of this book. To wit, for the first year meet at least once a month (more frequent meetings would be better, particularly in the first year) and practice making investment decisions by creating a fantasy portfolio. The members might even create an electronic communication process, using the Internet to share ideas and discoveries with one another during the interim between meetings.

At the end of that first year, give or take a few months, the club should be ready for launch. The prospective members will have probably become comfortable with the bookkeeping process, the investment philosophy of the club will have become crystallized, and they will have collectively identified a good number of reliable sources of research information available on the Internet. All of the members of the club should then have a high level of confidence that the initial contribution of $10,000 or more represents a prudent investment.

One important step that must be taken is the first step. That is, how do you find 25 people who have the necessary initial contribution and who also are capable of embracing this concept with enthusiasm? I would suggest that if you can't assemble these 25 people from you personal contacts, there are a couple of ideas that you might pursue. Before mentioning these alternatives, however, don't dismiss the possibility of building an investment club from your personal contacts. You don't have to know all 25 prospective members. Use the chain letter concept. You might know just 4 or 5 qualified participants, but each of those might also know 4 or 5 qualified participants. Consequently, the entire group of 25 members could be assembled as the result of 5 or 6 individuals making 4 or 5 phone calls.

There are at least two alternatives to this process. The first alternative is to contact the manager of a discount brokerage firm in your city. Explain what you want to do and ask his/her cooperation in introducing the concept to some of the brokerage firm's clients. Since investment clubs are likely to generate a good bit of supplemental business for that firm, they should be willing to cooperate with you. In fact, any Schwab or similar office would be wise to be proactive in this regard by initiating the formation of investment clubs among their clients.

The second alternative is to search the Internet for Chat Groups that are focused on investing. Simply announce to one of these groups what you are trying to accomplish and invite anyone who might be interested in the concept to contact you.

Most investment clubs are too conservative.

It's been my experience that most investment clubs are, in fact, too conservative with their investments. The fault with this is that you don't need to be a member of an investment club in order to invest in AT&T, IBM or any of the other components of the Dow Jones Industrial Average. You can make those investments on your own, outside of the club.

Perhaps a brief discussion concerning the amount of money that any investor should put at risk might be appropriate here. I don't believe that any investor should commit 100% of his/her available funds to the concepts proposed in this book, or to *any* individual stocks, whether they be blue chip or not. Why? The answer is that all stocks have an inherent level of risk. Recent market history offers ample evidence that even the bluest of blue chip stocks can lose money for investors. The exact percentage of total assets made available for investing in individual stocks is something that should be determined by each individual.

Having said that, I will suggest the following. Consider committing half of your total investment funds to the more aggressive concepts outlined in this book. What should be done with the other half of your investment assets? Again, that's a personal decision, but here's what I would recommend. Purchase an equity index fund. The evidence indicates that many investors are doing precisely that. According to AMG Data Services, more than 70% of the $24 billion that Americans put into equity mutual funds during the first quarter of 1999 went into index funds.

Most mutual funds and other institutional investors are necessarily committed to making investments in the larger corporations of America. There is no way that the average individual investor can gain any significant advantage in trying to compete with them in that arena. However, I'm convinced that you and I can compete very effectively with them in the arena outlined in this book.

Consequently, as mentioned earlier, I would recommend that you commit half of your funds to the Mainstay Equity Index Fund. It will provide pretty much the same performance as any of the other equity index funds, with the incremental advantage of guaranteeing against the possibility of ever losing any of your original investment if held for at least 10 years. Even if the market crashes, you are guaranteed by New York Life Insurance Co. that the full amount of your original investment will be repaid if the investment is held for a minimum of 10 years.

Knowing that at least half of your investment funds are almost totally free from risk (the only risk is the risk of loss of purchasing power caused by inflation) should enable you to assume a higher level of risk with the balance of your funds. If your group acquires an advanced level of competency in discovering investment opportunities, you should be able to achieve a substantially higher level of reward that will compensate for that higher level of risk.

Remember that the significant rewards in the world of investing go to the earliest discoverers of useful investment information. That's why investing in the AT&Ts and IBMs of the world is a losing proposition for most individual investors. You can't match the resources available to institutional investors in their quest to discover useful investment information about America's largest corporations. Knowing that your investment club has the potential to beat the performance of institutional investors by pursuing some of the concepts presented in this book will add to the interest and excitement.

The decision making process is too slow.

Meeting once a month to decide whether to buy General Motors or Eastman Kodak will not enhance anyone's investment skills. Markets today are very vibrant and move faster than they did when many of the old investment adages were coined. And yet, those adages continue to guide the thinking of many individual investors. My observation has been that many investment club members are more concerned about not violating those investment philosophies than they are about learning new and more effective methods for making investment decisions. Prudence, not profitability, is their primary objective.

Consequently they eschew some of the newer sources of information and some of the techniques that will enable them to achieve a competitive advantage over the larger institutional investors. In fact, their decision-making processes are very much like the institutional investors. Investment decisions are made at regular committee meetings rather than when new information becomes available.

Investment clubs should try to set up a communications structure that will enable them to make investment decisions more like these resourceful individual investors and less like the plodding institutional investors. If they fail to do this, they will lose perhaps the most important advantage that individual investors have over institutional investors: the ability to get in and out of the market quickly. This doesn't mean that individual investors or investment clubs should be focused purely on making a lot of trades. What it does mean is that they should have the capability of expeditiously responding to investment opportunities when they appear. If these clubs decide to debate the pros and cons of an investment for a couple of months they will likely miss the opportunity to maximize their investment returns.

One final note about the communication processes of investment clubs. Do you recall the comments about message boards in a previous chapter? Some day an enterprising individual will set up a home page on the Internet that will be used as a message board exclusively for investment clubs. As you may recall, message boards offer significant potential for individual investors, as well as for investment clubs. If your club discovers an emerging growth stock, then wouldn't it make sense for you to share that discovery with other investment clubs after your club has made its investment?

By the way, let me offer a parenthetical thought. This concept of dis-covering an investment opportunity, making an investment in that opportunity and then disseminating information about your discovery to other investors is precisely what the folks on Wall Street have been doing for years. When Wall Street came to Main Street, the real essence of that move was that a very effective network was created for dissemi-nating that sort of information and providing the folks on Wall Street with an abundant and seemingly endless flow of profits.

It might be considered presumptuous for anyone to suggest that investment clubs don't have sufficient funds for investing, are too conservative and have a decision-making process that is too slow. After all, the increase in the number of these clubs has been phenomenal. Well, a recent study by Terrance Odean and Brad M. Barber, finance professors at the Graduate School of Management at the University of California, Davis suggests that most investment clubs don't do that well. Their analysis of 166 investment clubs covering the period from February 1991 and January 1997 revealed that the average annual return for those clubs was just 14.1%, or over 3 percentage points lower than the overall market!

The antithesis of the adage–*If it ain't broker, don't fix it*–might be appropriate here. It appears that the current methodology of many investment clubs is generating results that do not match the performance of the overall market. Perhaps one remedy for those poorer performing funds might be to adopt some of the concepts presented in this book!

An Alternative for the Average Investor–Retirement Funds

Today's work force is full of newly minted 401(k) fat cats, cashing in on better benefits and a still-sizzling stock market. One out of every five accounts these days has passed the $100,000 mark. And with plan assets swelling $5,000 a second, the person in the next cubicle might actually be a millionaire.

Newsweek, May 31, 1999, page 77

For many people their retirement fund represents the lion's share of their overall investment wealth. Almost all of that money is invested in passive investments, specifically, in mutual funds. While some companies have expanded the number of mutual funds that can be selected, participants are almost always constrained to choose passive investments. In most cases the only opportunity that 401(k) investors have to invest in individual stocks is when they opt to invest some of their funds in their employer's stock. A few forward-looking companies have begun to allow participants to trade individual securities.

I'm not aware of any reason why participants in 401(k) plans can't apply the concepts espoused in this book towards their retirement nest eggs. The fact that some companies currently allow 401(k) participants to trade in individual stocks supports this possibility. If necessary, companies might even encourage individuals to demonstrate their ability to build portfolio value by first creating their own fantasy portfolios, thereby proving or disproving their ability to make profitable investment decisions. If those efforts succeed in beating the performance of the market, then those individuals are likely to feel very comfortable about allocating part or all of their 401(k) assets to the discovery and purchase of emerging growth stocks as outlined in this book.

Furthermore, if investment clubs offer individual investors the opportunity to lower risk and increase returns, then why can't that concept be applied to retirement funds? Why can't 10 or 15 people covered by the same retirement fund pool their resources to achieve those same objectives? Companies may balk at offering this option to employees, offering the excuse that record-keeping would be far too complicated. In fact, many mutual funds are selected by HR departments primarily because of their ability to provide essential individual participant records.

The National Association of Investors Corp. has developed and refined an accounting system that accommodates unequal investment contributions as well as how to compute fair values for new and departing members. This system was developed specifically for investment clubs, but could readily be used for the pooling of retirement funds.

Summary and Conclusion

Having spent almost three years working my own fantasy portfolio, I am convinced that the essential processes that enabled me to increase the value of that portfolio from $250,000 to over $9 million in less than 3 years are contained within this book.

Although the chapter on financial controls may seem dry and perhaps a bit boring, it is an important part of the learning process. Try to be diligent about keeping good records. That's the only way that you can accurately measure your personal learning progress. More important, it's absolutely and emphatically necessary when you venture into the world of investing with real money.

The more I work with and think about the two methods for discovering growth stocks–using quarterly earnings announcements and daily analysis of extraordinary trading activity–the more convinced I've become that they are exceptionally valuable tools. I have become particularly convinced of the value derived from the extraordinary trading activity.

In mid-December, 1999, I liquidated my entire portfolio with the exception of one stock. Roughly three weeks later, over a period of 2-3 days, I re-built my portfolio to a full complement of 15 stocks. What is remarkable is that it soon became difficult to make decisions about which stocks to remove to make room for new candidates. You may recall that making those decisions is sort of the litmus test to measure the progress that you're making. Using the extraordinary trading volume methodology you will have no difficulty in finding new stocks.

One final note. I want to re-emphasize the importance of reading selective financial newspapers and magazines. One of the secrets in discovering emerging growth stocks is this: If you've done a good job of trying to understand the economy, learning which industry segments represent the best opportunity for growth and what the challenges are within those industries, you will experience a visceral charge when one of the two discovery methods reveals a company that has provided answers to those challenges.

An actual experience with my fantasy portfolio will illustrate this point. About two years ago I read of a company–Superconductor Technology Inc. (SCON)–that was developing cryogenic filters for the wireless communications industry. Two of the benefits derived from SCON filters operating at very low temperatures are that transmission is clearer and there are fewer dropped calls. However, it was a technology that was ahead of the market. Wireless communication company owners weren't motivated to invest in this equipment since their current equipment was adequate.

The consequence was that SCON stock never traded above $5 or $6 per share for the next couple of years. Then, toward the end of 1999 many of the technology journals and some of the business magazines began to publish stories about the emergence of wireless broadband transmission. Whereas analog and digital wireless transmission could make do with the existing filters, broadband transmission would require the higher operating efficiencies promised by SCON's filters. In early 2000 (late January or early February) SCON appeared on the BigChart list of Nasdaq stocks with the greatest percentage increase in volume. That was the trigger event.

I added 40,000 shares to my fantasy portfolio at $12 per share. Within two weeks the stock was trading at better than $65 per share.

Obviously very few stocks will generate that type of performance. However, this experience demonstrates the efficacy of two practices suggested in this book:

1. Use the BigCharts and Bar Chart sources of information. Both are excellent mechanisms for timing your investment decisions.

2. Focus on a specific industry segment and do as much research about that industry as your time permits. This research will help you to respond quickly and with confidence when you spot a familiar stock that appears in one of those two sources.

Chapter 5

The Necessary Financial Controls

"In The New Market Wizards, Jack Schwager warns investors: 'Do your own thinking…never listen to the opinions of others.' And those 'experts' include money managers, brokers, planners…and financial newsletters.
Never rely on their advice to make your investment decisions, the performance of 90 percent of money managers falls short of the S&P 500 Index, and most newsletters are just as bad if not worse. At least 90 percent are losers. Trust no one, do it yourself."
CBS Market Watch–Paul B. Farrell: Never rely on newsletter for advice 7-23-98

"By improving the base of your investment knowledge, better outcomes are ensured. After all, even baseball's homerun Kings, Mark McGwire and Sammy Sosa, take batting practice. Without work on the fundamentals, success cannot be guaranteed."
The New Era of Wealth, by Brian Wesbury, p. 11

Imagine that you have just received a make-believe gift of $250,000.
Aside from being imaginary, this is a special gift. It represents the beginning of a learning process that will improve your ability to make money
in the stock market. As you become immersed in this challenge, you will
find that it is mentally stimulating and it will stir your competitive
juices. Best of all, it's fun...and it's free.

I strongly encourage you to diligently comply with the following
guidelines:

1. The $250,000 can only be used to create an investment port-
    folio that will consist of nothing other than common
    stocks–and cash.
2. That portfolio can *never* contain more than 15 stocks.
3. Initially, the portfolio will be equal dollar weighted–you will
    invest roughly $16,500 in each of your first 15 stock selections.
4. All of the investment decisions, initially and for as long as you
    manage your fantasy portfolio, should to be made solely by you.
5. Using the financial controls described later in this chapter, you
    have to keep bullet-proof records of all the buy and sell transac-
    tions that you make in your portfolio.

If the above five conditions are faithfully followed, you will almost
certainly emerge from this hands-on experience with a higher level of
confidence in your ability to select stocks. The level of knowledge you
will acquire, and the degree of success you experience in managing your
imaginary $250,000 portfolio, will be determined purely by the time,
focus and enthusiasm that you commit to the project.

Remember that, at least in the beginning, this exercise is intended to
help you learn how to use the Internet and other complementary
sources to make investment decisions for your imaginary $250,000
portfolio. None of your own money will be at risk. If you have precon-
ceived notions about the risks of investing in common stocks, try to put
such thoughts out of your mind. Approach this challenge with the
frame of mind that you have a lot to gain–the opportunity to increase

your investment knowledge/ investment skills–and nothing, other than time, to lose.

How much time will be necessary? This will be dictated by your own personal circumstances. This program has been designed to provide you with plenty of flexibility insofar as time is concerned. However, if you decide that you sincerely want to go through a productive learning experience, I would suggest that you spend no less than two hours per week on this project. That's the amount of time that you should dedicate to discovering new investment opportunities and also to maintaining proper records.

Because of the vibrant nature of the information on the Internet, you don't have to consider the commitment of this time as being an inconvenience or a burden. In fact, because there is so much stimulating and useful investment information on the Internet, some of you will wish you could commit more time to surfing. If you have a genuine interest in discovering investment opportunities that can increase your wealth, you're definitely going to enjoy this program.

Are the Five Conditions Necessary?

In a word, "Yes!" Here's why.

Condition #1: Your imaginary $250,000 can only be used to create an investment portfolio that will consist of nothing other than common stocks and cash.

Why should your investments be restricted to common stocks? The answer is quite elementary: Of all conventional investment alternatives, common stocks have provided investors with the highest rate of return over extended periods of time.

For example, during the past 25 years there have been only five years when the overall market, as measured by the S&P 500 Index, has declined in value. Three of those declines occurred within the first five years of this 25-year period. For the past 10 years (1990 through 1999) the S&P 500 Index has increased at a compound annual rate of 17.8%. Putting real dollars into that performance, if you had invested $10,000 in the S&P 500 Index at the beginning of 1989, that original investment would have grown to $51,624 by the end of 1999.

You might ask, "What level of risk will I be exposed to by investing in stocks"? An answer to that question is offered by a chart found on page 343 of Burton G. Malkiel's book *A Random Walk Down Wall Street*. The chart is entitled "Range of Annual Returns on Common Stocks for Various Time Periods, 1950-88." During that 39-year period, the worst one-year return was a loss of 26.5%. The best return was a gain of 52.6%. If anyone is considering making an investment in stocks with money that will be needed within one year, those numbers offer an historic insight relative to the potential one-year risks and rewards–at least for that 39-year period of time.

Look at those statistics from a different perspective. Let's assume that at some time during the time period from 1950 to 1988 you had some surplus cash that you were going to need at the end of one year. You decided to invest that money in a market index fund (they didn't exist until the late 1970s or early 1980s, but let's pretend that they did). If you had been extraordinarily lucky, you might have been invested during a year when the market generated a 52.6% gain. If you had been extraordinarily unlucky, you might have been invested during a year when the market lost 26.5% of its value–which is roughly what you would have lost.

The next statistic lends a lot of credibility to the advice that many financial planners offer to investors: don't invest any funds in stocks if you will need those funds within the next five years. For any five-year period from 1950–1988 (for example, 1950 to 1954, 1951 to 1955, 1952 to 1956, etc.) the worst performance was an average annual loss of 2.4% per year. The best five-year performance was an average annual gain of 23.9% per year. Most investors would be willing to assume that level of potential risk (-2.4% per year) to achieve that level of potential gain (23.9% per year). The average annual gain for all five-year periods (1950-54 through 1984-88) was about 10% per year.

Finally, investors with a time horizon of 10 years or greater had no risk at all during this 39-year period. All ten-year or greater time periods (1950-59 through 1979-88) generated positive returns. As the time horizons increased beyond 10 years, the upper limit returns decreased and the lower limit returns increased. The average annual return for all time periods was approximately 10%.

Condition #2: Your portfolio can never contain more than 15 stocks.

Diversification is an important concept since there are two extremes: too many stocks and too few. One of the reasons that roughly 80% to 90% of all mutual funds and all investment managers under-perform the market averages is that their portfolios contain too many stocks.

It's rare that all of the stocks in a portfolio rise in value at the same time. In fact, it's quite likely that not all of the stocks in a portfolio will rise in value. What is more likely is that most of the stocks will generate "average" performance or decrease in value while one or two will "shoot the lights out."

This is a phenomenon that seems to be characteristic of all portfolios—even such conservative benchmark portfolios as the S&P 500. Ibbotson Associates, a Chicago research firm that specializes in market analysis, calculated what the S&P's return would have been over the past dozen years if the top 50 performers (just 10% of the total) were eliminated from the list. The result of their study indicated that the index's annual gain would have been almost half of what was actually reported. Viewed from a different perspective, 10% of the stocks were responsible for almost doubling the performance of the index! (See *The Wall Street Journal*, 9/15/97, "Trying to Pick Highfliers Can Prove to be Perilous.")

It's important to guard against putting too many stocks in your portfolio since too many stocks can dilute performance. Why? Let's use an illustration. Assume that we have two portfolios, each with $1 million invested in stocks. Portfolio A starts with $100,000 invested in each of 10 stocks. Portfolio B starts with $20,000 invested in each of 50 stocks. Each portfolio has one stock that doubles in value, while all the other

stocks in the portfolio remain unchanged. The consequence to
Portfolio A of having one stock double in market value is that the overall portfolio value will have increased by 10%, while Portfolio B's value
will have been increased by just 2%.

Most portfolio managers can find a few stocks that offer strong, compelling financial characteristics–stocks that offer the potential to double
in value or more. Adding these stocks to their portfolios is a relatively
easy decision. Eventually these decisions will be relatively easy for you
as well. However, as the number of stocks in a portfolio is increased, the
"compelling financial characteristics" of each incremental stock
selected become less compelling.

Nevertheless, the less appealing stocks are added to portfolios for two
reasons. First, even stocks with "compelling financial characteristics"
are vulnerable to unexpected negative surprises and subsequent
declines in market value. Second, diversification decreases the
probability that poor performance from one or two stocks will
negatively impact the overall portfolio performance. Therefore, for
most professional portfolio managers the "quantity" of stocks selected
for a portfolio becomes almost as important as the "quality" of stocks.

The reason for this is quite fundamental. As important as superior
investment performance might be to investment managers and mutual
fund managers, it is not as important as avoiding negative investment
returns. Individual and institutional investors are far more tolerant of
below-average positive returns than they are of negative returns. For
example, if the overall market is up 25% and an investment manager or
mutual fund manager's performance is up only 15%, that 15% increase
in portfolio value is more acceptable to investors than even a 1%
decrease in portfolio value.

The other extreme in diversification is having too few stocks. There is
never going to be an opportunity to invest in a stock that is completely
risk-free, especially in a competitive economy. Consequently, portfolios
with fewer stocks present a higher risk than portfolios with a larger

number of stocks. For individual investors and for investment clubs, the ideal number of stocks within a portfolio is probably somewhere between 15 and 20. That number of stocks provides the opportunity for better than average appreciation while simultaneously diminishing risk. Equally important, smaller portfolios are more manageable both in terms of the selection process and in terms of the critical process of monitoring the performance of individual stocks within the portfolio. However, perhaps the most important benefit derives from the fact that limiting the portfolio to 15 stocks will discipline you to be more critical about which stocks you select.

As you get started with this exercise, you're going to feel somewhat like a kid in a candy store. You will discover a lot of stocks with terrific stories that you will want to include in your portfolio. If there were no limitations on the number of stocks, it would be quite simple to dump every one of these irresistible stocks into your portfolio. Limiting the portfolio to 15 stocks will force you to become more disciplined, and hopefully more prudently selective, in making investment decisions.

Actually, the decision to add a stock to a portfolio is probably the easiest decision that you will have to make. As you become more skilled in screening stocks you're going to discover that the really difficult part of managing your portfolio will be trying to decide which of the existing 15 stocks in your portfolio should be removed!

Why is this likely? Because as your selection skills improve, the quality of the stocks added to the portfolio will also improve. After a period of time, your portfolio will consist of 15 stocks that, in your judgment, have the greatest potential for meeting your investment goals. This process will necessarily force you to focus more clearly on your investment goals. Questions will arise in your mind, such as "What are my investment objectives?" and "Which of these stocks best meet those goals?" As you search for answers to these questions, you'll discover that your research efforts will also become more focused and, hopefully, more profitable. This process becomes a wonderfully reinforcing cycle resulting in an overall improvement in your ability to make profitable investment decisions.

A couple of final thoughts. As you get started with your portfolio(s) don't be hesitant about adding and deleting stocks. The Prudent Man investment theory doesn't apply to this process. Remember that it's designed to be a learning experience and you're working with play money. You can accelerate the learning process if you keep an investment diary in which you record your reasons for adding and deleting stocks from your portfolio. This would be especially helpful memory jogger when you have to make a decision about which of the 15 stocks in the portfolio should be removed to make room for a new addition.

I would also encourage you to keep a list of stocks that have been deleted from your portfolio and periodically review the performance of those stocks. If any of those stocks increase in market value after they were deleted, part of the learning process is to discover why they increased. If they decline in value or don't change much, that observation will reinforce your reasons for eliminating them from the portfolio.

Condition #3: Initially your portfolio will be "equal dollar weighted"–each of your first 15 selections will be allocated approximately $16,500.

The reason for this condition is closely related to Condition #2. Because you can't be certain which of the 15 stocks in your portfolio might "shoot the lights out," it's a good idea to place your bets evenly. There is a further reason for this level of distribution. Allocating a larger dollar amount to certain stocks is a bit like using leverage. When you use leverage, most of your money is invested in a stock that you think will perform well. If the stock subsequently increases in value, then you'll feel justified in making that decision. However, if the stock decreases in value the subsequent loss will be greater than if you had made an "equal dollar weighted" investment.

Let's use some real numbers to illustrate that phenomenon. Assume that you decided to invest half of your $250,000 initial value in just one stock, and spread the remaining $125,000 among 14 other stocks. If that one stock increased by 25% and all the other stocks remained unchanged, your overall portfolio would increase by $31,250 or by 12.5%. On the other hand, if that stock declined by 25% and all the other stocks remained unchanged, your overall portfolio would decrease by $31,250, or by 12.5%. In contrast, if your portfolio were equal-dollar weighted, you would have invested roughly $16,500 in each stock. Now a 25% change in the value of that one stock–while all other stocks remained unchanged–would result in just a $4,125 increase or decrease in the overall portfolio value, or just a 1.65% gain or loss. Leverage is a double-edged sword!

Over time the dollar value of each of the 15 stocks in your portfolio will change. Some stocks will increase in value, some will decrease and some will stay the same. One of the strategies that you might want to consider is to periodically rebalance the portfolio. You can do this by selling some shares of your winners and buying some shares of your losers. The end result should be that each of the 15 stocks once again has been roughly allocated an equal number of dollars. How often should you rebalance the portfolio? You can make that judgment on your own. However, probably once a year will be enough.

An exception to that rebalancing frequency might arise if one or two of your stocks doubles or triples in value and you decide to take profits. If that occurs, you might want to then adjust the entire portfolio. In other words, after selling the one or two stocks, compute the total value of the portfolio and divide that amount by 15. Let's assume that the overall portfolio value has increased to $300,000. If you are going to be adding two new stocks to the portfolio, the previous computation will dictate that $20,000 ($300,000 divided by 15 stocks) should be invested in each stock. You can then scan the remaining 13 stocks to determine whether or not to purchase additional shares to bring their market value up to $20,000.

Another scenario that could develop is that you might select a stock that will accelerate very rapidly in market value–perhaps doubling, or more, in less than a year. If and when you have the good fortune of experiencing that, you might want to sell half of your position in that stock. For example, if you have 800 shares of a $20 stock and the market value of that stock catapults to $40 per share within a short period of time, sell 400 shares and keep the remaining 400 shares. Since you've recovered your original investment with the sale of the 400 shares, your cost for the remaining 400 shares is essentially zero. The cash generated from this sale can be used to add to other positions or just kept in cash, depending on your assessment of market valuations at that time.

Condition #4: "All of your selections, initially and for as long as you manage your fantasy portfolio, have to be made solely by you."

You're not going to learn as much about investing from this experience if you select stocks by calling your broker for ideas or if you ask anyone for recommendations–and then ignore the responsibility for doing your own research to be sure that the investment idea meets your requirements. Remember that the purpose of this exercise is to enable you to access and use the growing number of investment information sources on the Internet so that you can make your own investment decisions.

Condition #5: "Using the financial controls described in Chapter 4, you have to keep 'bullet-proof' records of all additions to and deletions from your portfolio."

The mechanics for achieving this and the reasons for its importance will be covered later in this chapter.

A Very Inexpensive Education

It's very difficult for most people to be unemotional about their own money. The emotions of greed and fear are almost always present when investing and they can be distracting, if not damaging, to investment performance. In fact, these emotions are so ubiquitous and potent that they often strongly influence entire markets. What other explanation could there be for substantial market movements, up or down, that occur within the span of a few days–or even a few hours? Do the fundamental economic conditions change that quickly? Probably not, other than with a decision by the Federal Reserve Board to increase or lower interest rates. Many would argue that the market has anticipated even those changes. The more probable explanation for dramatic reversals in market trends is that mass psychology–not basic economics–has changed from greed to fear or from fear to greed.

Most of us work hard to generate the surplus funds that can be used for investing. We feel a sense of exhilaration when our invested "nest eggs" increase in value. We become sideline cheerleaders, silently imploring the market to continue rising. As the market moves higher, greed motivates more individuals to invest. Nobody wants to be standing on the platform after the train to increased wealth has departed from the station. Ah, but what a different set of emotions overcomes us when the market starts to reduce the size of our "nest egg"! Initially we may just be annoyed. But as the market continues to decline, annoyance turns to frustration and eventually to panic. It soon becomes so unbearable that we decide to cut our losses and sell.

Professional investors know very well that the secret to successful investing is to buy low and sell high. Since for every buyer there must be a seller and for every seller there must be a buyer, it's axiomatic that all investors can't buy at the same time nor can they all sell at the same time. Therefore you won't find too many professional investors buying when a sense of euphoria has engulfed the markets. They're more likely to be sellers. At the other end of the emotional spectrum, guess who's buying when everyone else is panicking? That's right–those savvy professional investors. They know that our economy isn't going to self-destruct. They know that our system of capitalism will survive almost any form of calamity. The panic selling of the masses provides them with the opportunity to re-enter the market. Buy low. Sell high. Got it!

One of the by-products of the system suggested in this book is that it has the potential to remove the emotional factors from the world of investing. You'll still experience a sense of frustration every now and then because your decisions will not always be good decisions. However, because your hard-earned savings aren't being jeopardized, you are not likely to get either euphoric over gains or despondent over losses. Your ego may get a boost when you've made some good decisions. However, it's not as painful when the market value of your make-believe portfolio declines as it would be if this were real money.

The virtue of eliminating some of the emotion from investing is that you can learn a lot more about investing if your emotions aren't involved. When emotions aren't distorting your analysis of the market, you can learn a lot more about its rhythms. For example, if your portfolio drops 20% or more within the span of a week or two, you'll learn that you don't have to panic. Rather, you can do one of two things.

First, you can ride out the storm, knowing that the market is probably going to recover. Comfort yourself by understanding that even if it doesn't, what have you lost? It's make-believe money! The fact that it probably will recover will provide you with the necessary knowledge and strength to ride out similar declines in the future when you're using real money. Second, you can take this opportunity to re-arrange your portfolio by buying some of those stocks that you watched soar in value before you had a chance to add them to your portfolio. When markets correct, those big winners usually give up a lot of their gains and come down to a more affordable level. The market correction will provide you with an opportunity to invest in these proven winners. Then, when the market ultimately begins another period of rising prices, you'll feel pretty smart because you'll now be invested in some of the market leaders.

You'll probably also come to understand why markets and stocks are sometimes very volatile. A lot of investors can be categorized as momentum investors. They don't do the necessary research that is recommended in this book. Rather, they just observe the dynamics of the marketplace. If they're convinced that stocks and/or markets are trending higher, they invest. The reason this type of investing creates volatility is that when markets begin to change course, even for a mild correction, momentum investors are usually the first ones to sell.

Why? Remember that they invested in a particular stock only because they observed that a lot of other investors were doing the same thing. They went along for the ride. When the upward trend of prices hesitates or turns down, the momentum investors want to secure their profits. Because they didn't do their own research, they have no idea of what the potential future market value of a stock might be. Nor do they care to know! In contrast, investors who have done their homework can afford the comfort of being long-term investors, knowing that any dips in market values are normal and certainly not a cause for panic.

The lessons that you will learn by eliminating or controlling the emotions of fear and greed can prove to be extremely valuable to you when you are eventually investing real money.

Should You Always be Fully Invested?

Are there times when more of your assets should be in cash rather than stocks? The simple answer is "Yes." The market moves in both directions—up and down. Since most stock gain value when the market goes up, it's obviously better to have more of your money in stocks and less in cash when the market goes up. Since most stock lose value when the market goes down, it's obviously better to have more of your money in cash and less in stocks when the market goes down.

If you could anticipate market reversals and make the appropriate adjustments in your portfolio, your investment performance would be significantly higher than simply buying and holding stocks. But this begs the question: "How do you know when the market is going to go down...or up?" One of the adages that every stockbroker learns early in his/her career is the following: "Nobody blows a whistle to announce the beginning of a rise or fall in the market." The issue being addressed here is that of market timing.

There have been many articles and books about the virtues of market timing. These publications have been authored by people within the industry and by academics. Their incontrovertible conclusion is that market timing simply does not work.

Financial Controls

Many investors think they are pretty astute at picking mutual funds, selecting individual stocks and calling market turns. Yet a lot of these folks don't know for sure, because they don't track their portfolios.

The Wall Street Journal, June 23, 1998, "Getting Going" by Jonathan Clemens

For some of you this will be the most difficult part of managing your imaginary portfolio. If you are already reasonably proficient with Microsoft Excel, the financial controls proposed in this section will be a breeze. If you're not proficient with Excel–or a similar spreadsheet format–you should be able to get by with the directions offered here. If you prefer to create your own financial control sheets, I would encourage you to get a primer on Excel to facilitate your getting started with this program. As you advance into the program, using these financial controls will become a snap for all of you.

You're going to need some financial controls in order to manage your portfolio effectively. Like any competitive endeavor–and make no mistake about it, investing is a competitive endeavor–you will need a system for keeping score. You can probably follow some of the suggestions in this book without using the recommended financial controls, but doing so would be somewhat like playing in a golf tournament without keeping score. You won't have an accurate measure of how good or how bad your overall performance has been.

In the game of golf, most of us amateurs can experience the thrill of occasional near-perfect strokes during an 18-hole outing. Those are the strokes that we contemplate after the round has been completed. Overlooked are the inept strokes that clearly outnumbered the few perfect ones. Investors have a similar mentality. We tend to focus on the investments we made that resulted in the greatest increase in market value–the investments that gave us a warm glow of satisfaction. Ignored are the "dogs" that resulted in flat performance or losses. Those investments don't disappear simply because we don't think about them as much as we think about our winning investments.

Certainly there are reasons for investing other than financial gain. As with those perfect strokes in golf, perhaps we're satisfied, even exultant, about the occasional "home run" we achieve with our investment decisions. Or, perhaps investing is an avocation–a hobby or simply an entertaining diversion. However, if your objective in investing is to increase your personal wealth, then you absolutely must gain access to a system that will enable you to measure your overall investment return profile.

Why is that important? Because if your overall rate of return is poor, then you might want to consider changing your investment strategy. How can you determine whether your overall investment results are acceptable? Quite simply, there are alternatives to making your own investment decisions for your stock portfolio. At the very least, your investment performance should be better than the rate your money could earn by investing in government bonds. The rate of return won't be very exciting, but if your investment performance in stocks is consistently lower than what you could have earned by investing in the comparatively "risk-free" government bonds, then perhaps that's where you ought to put your money.

If, on the other hand, you want to participate in the historically higher returns of stocks–and you're willing to accept the inherent risks–then perhaps you ought to consider investing in one of the index funds that are offered by mutual fund companies.

This purpose of this book is to offer you another alternative. I'm convinced that it is possible for amateur investors to learn how to make investment decisions that will beat the performance of the market. Should you opt for this alternative, however, measuring performance becomes even more important.

Here are some of the tools that will help you to measure your investment performance:

A *Control Sheet* in which every "buy" and "sell" transaction can be registered. This tool will be very important in helping you to determine the number of shares you can afford to buy at any given point in time.

A *Valuation Sheet* that will enable you to record the weekly or monthly (your choice–my preference is weekly) valuations of your portfolio, along with the valuation of an appropriate benchmark.

A *Performance Chart* that will enable you to plot the performance of your portfolio and the selected benchmark over extended periods of time. Since most "benchmarks" (Dow Jones Industrial Average, S&P 500, etc.) are measured from the beginning of each year, that's how you will eventually want to measure the performance of your portfolio.

Each of these documents can be created using Microsoft Excel or an alternative spread sheet format. In the charts that appear at the end of this chapter, the numbers and letters at the top and along the left side of each chart–the numbers and letters with a gray background–refer to the column (letters) and row (numbers) designations used in Microsoft Excel.

The Control Sheet

The Control Sheet is *always* the first point of entry when adding or removing a stock from your portfolio. When you are just beginning, you will just be adding the initial 15 stocks to your portfolio. Thereafter, you must first enter the data for the stock that is being removed and then enter the data for the new stock being added. The reason for that sequence is that you won't know how much cash will be available for the new addition until you compute the cash proceeds from the stock being removed.

There are several benefits derived from the use of this Control Sheet. First of all, the "Cost" column (G) and the "Receipt" column (J) can be set up to automatically total all entries within each category. You can start this procedure after you have made your first stock selection. To set up this automatic computation, click on the cell directly below the "Cost" cell (G4). In the formula bar (the area where the information to be placed in the selected cell appears), type the following: =(E4*F4)+8.

The E4 and the F4 refer to the specific cell locations within the Excel grid. In our illustration, the E refers to Column E, or the number of shares purchased, and the F refers to the price per share of the purchase. The 4 refers to the Row in your Excel sheet where the transaction is being recorded. The * denotes a multiplication function, and the 8 represents the hypothetical $8 commission for your online transaction. Once the formula has been recorded in the formula bar, hit "Enter" and the total cost for that particular transaction will be recorded automatically in the cell originally selected (G4). It won't be necessary to enter this formula every time you add a stock to your portfolio. When additional stocks are added, simply select that first cell (G4), place the cursor on the lower right corner of the cell until a plus sign is formed and drag the cursor down to the next cell. The formula will be automatically entered in that cell. This click and drag method can be used for copying the formula in any contiguous cell, whether that cell is above or below the cell that is being copied.

Repeat this process using the appropriate cell designations for automatically computing "Receipts" in Column J. However, there will be a slight modification. Select cell J4. Once that cell has become highlighted, enter the following formula in the formula bar: =(E4*I4)-8.

This formula represents the number of shares being sold (E4) times the market value of each share (I4) minus the $8 online commission.

To automatically compute the total amount of all purchases, click in the "Totals / Cost" cell (G44). Click on the Auto Sum button on the toolbar, click on cell G4 and drag the cursor down to the last cell before the "Total / Cost" cell (G43). Repeat this process for the "Receipt" column and, at the appropriate time in the future, for the total in the "Net Gain (Loss)" column.

The final step for fully automating this page is to establish a formula for the "Net Gain (Loss)" column. Highlight cell K4. Enter the following formula in the formula bar: =J4-G4

Hit "Enter." Once again, this formula can be duplicated in any cell by either highlighting and dragging for contiguous cells or copying (Control C) and pasting (Control V) for non-contiguous cells within the same column.

A few words of caution are necessary. If you have entered the formulae and applied it to all rows within each of the three columns, this may create some misinformation. For example, if you have acquired a stock for the portfolio and have not yet liquidated that position, two problems arise. First, the "Receipt" column for that particular entry will record a negative "8." To eliminate that entry, select that cell, select "Edit" from the tool bar and then "Clear" and "Content." The formula can be re-created when necessary by selecting and dragging from a *contiguous* cell–or selecting, copying and pasting from a *non-contiguous* cell–containing the formula within that column.

The second problem will occur in the "Net Gain (Loss)" column. Even though you still have the stock in your portfolio, the entry for this column will register a *loss* equal to the "Total Cost" and the negative "8" from the "Receipt" column computation. Once again, go through the Edit, Clear, Contents process to rectify this situation.

In addition to ensuring that you will not make any computational errors, setting up these formulae is very useful in computing and verifying the amount of cash available at any given time. Just follow the following process:

1) Add 250,000 to the amount in cell J44. The rationale behind this computation is that you began the portfolio with $250,000 in cash. When you sell any stock, the proceeds from the sale represent an increase in the amount of available cash.

2) Subtract the dollar amount obtained in step 1 from cell G44. Here again the logic is pretty straightforward. When you add a stock to your portfolio you decrease the amount of cash that is available.

Steps 1 and 2 can be automated by selecting cell J45 and entering the following in the formula bar:

$$=(J44+250,000)-G44$$

3) The resulting amount will represent the amount of cash that is available. If this computation results in a negative figure, you have spent too much money! If so, go back and reduce the number of shares that you have just acquired.

This step is very useful in determining the cash available for any new additions to your portfolio. When you've made a decision to add a new stock, the first thing to do is to enter the "Removed" data for the stock that is being deleted from the portfolio. After that information has been entered, cell J45 will automatically be updated with the amount of cash that is available for the new investment. To determine how many shares can be acquired, divide the cost per share of the new stock into the cash available. After entering all of the data for the new stock, once again cell J45 will be updated with the *new* level of cash in the portfolio. Be absolutely sure to enter that amount in the "Cash" cell (I20) of the *Weekly Valuation* sheet. Neglecting to make that entry will have an impact on the overall performance of your portfolio.

If one of the stocks in your current portfolio experiences a stock split, an adjustment entry will be required in the Control Sheet. For example, if XYZ Corporation declares a two-for-one stock split, your portfolio will then have twice as many shares of XYZ Corp. However, your overall cost will remain the same, which means that the *cost per share* will be half as much as the original cost. The best way to treat stock splits is to enter a new row (Insert/Row) just below the existing row for the stock that has been split. Enter the number of shares that will be distributed to you. For example, in the case of a 2/1 split, you would enter the same number of shares in the new row as you had in the previous row. The total cost of the new shares should be zero. It would be helpful if you would enter the date of the split and add a notation that the entry reflects a split.

In addition to providing a method for keeping track of the "cash" portion of your portfolio, the Control Sheet will provide you with a valuable source of information for computing your capital gains for income tax purposes. Once again, the magic of Microsoft Excel can expedite this process. First, depress Control and hold–then click on the name of the sheet at the bottom of the your computer screen. Once the + sign appears, drag to the right to create a copy of your Control Sheet chart. Next, select cell A1, hold down the left mouse button and drag the cursor diagonally across the chart until all of the cells within the chart have been selected. Release the left mouse button. Click on "Data" in the Tool Bar, click on "Sort", select the column in which "Date Sold" appears (H), select either "Ascending" or "Descending" and hit "Enter." Finally, you can highlight and erase all sales that did not appear in the year for which you're computing taxes. What's left will be a very convenient table that you can use for computing your overall investment capital gains or losses for that year.

The Control Sheet introduces the ingredient of discipline to the process of portfolio management. Discipline and financial controls provide the foundation for successful portfolio management. Without them, it would be extremely difficult, if not impossible, to accurately measure the performance of your investments. If you can't, or won't, comply with these requirements, your efforts to manage a portfolio could become an exercise in frustration.

The Valuation Sheet

Whenever any changes are made in your portfolio, the Valuation Sheet is the second document that you will have to modify. If you've removed a stock from the Control Sheet, then it must also be removed from the valuation sheet. Similarly, if you add a stock on the Control Sheet, then it must also be added to the Valuation Sheet.

The Valuation Sheet is the most important tool that you will need to assess the performance of your portfolio. Inasmuch as it will normally require less than a half-hour to update, I would encourage you to do this weekly. This tool will provide you with the visceral charge that will motivate you to strive for better performance. It is, if you will, your weekly report card. The Valuation Sheet will eliminate the guesswork relative to whether your portfolio's performance is above or below-average.

Some of the important features contained in this document are as follows:

⇒ There are a number of sources for generating closing prices (Column H) for your individual stock holdings. The most arduous of these sources would be one of the financial newspapers (*Barron's* would probably be the best, since it's available Saturday morning and it's very comprehensive). However, I've found that the best source is one of the online sources that enables you to create and monitor your own portfolio, such as My Yahoo. The virtue of using the valuations available from your portfolio page in My Yahoo is that the data is available a lot sooner than newspaper sources. In addition, since My Yahoo also totals the value of all of your stock holdings, this provides a check to the accuracy of your own calculations in Column I.

⇒ As in the Control Sheet, automatic computation is an important attribute of the Valuation Sheet. In this instance you can

establish the formula to create Column I by placing the cursor
and highlighting cell I4. In the formula bar, enter the following
formula: =G4*H4.

⇒ Once entered, highlight I4, place the cursor in the lower right
corner of that cell, wait for the plus sign to appear and drag the
cursor down to I18. All that remains to be done for computing
individual total values for each stock is simply entering the per
share values from My Yahoo. When updating this report on a
weekly basis, highlight cells H4 thru H18, select Edit, Clear and
Contents. The report will then be ready to accept and compute
the new weekly valuations. Actually, it isn't necessary to remove
the per share values from the prior week. Simply select the
appropriate cell and input the new per share market value. This
will automatically replace the prior week's value.

⇒ Click on cell I19 and then click on the Auto Sum figure in the
toolbar. Be sure that a flashing/dotted line has encompassed
cells I4 through I18. Hit Enter. The total current market value of
the stocks in the portfolio will automatically appear in I19.

The cash available in your portfolio will be entered in cell I20. It's
unlikely that you will always have all of your available funds invested in
stocks–there will almost always be some amount of cash in your total
portfolio value. When you first embark on this exercise, that amount
will be $250,000. As explained in the section on the Control Sheet, the
amount of cash available at any given point in time can and should be
calculated. Ignoring or miscalculating the amount of cash available will
have an impact on the performance of your portfolio. If you ignore it,
the performance might be overstated or understated.

Although I haven't provided a form for recording this, any cash dividends paid by companies within your portfolio should be added to the
cash position. If your focus is on small to mid-size companies in the
Infotech industry, as mine is, then there is no need to be concerned

about cash dividends. Most of these companies are ""cash hungry" and therefore pay no dividends.

⇒Click on cell I21. Select the Auto Sum icon from the tool bar and be sure that only cells I19 and I20 have been included. Hit Enter. The total value of your portfolio–stocks and cash–will appear in cell I21.

Whether you're investing in mutual funds or individual stocks, it's very important to determine whether your investment choices generate above or below-average performance. Unless you're pursuing investments as an avocation or as a learning experience, there simply is no reason why you should be willing to accept below-average performance. If you are pursuing an investment strategy of investing in small to medium cap high-tech stocks, perhaps the best benchmark to use would be the NASDAQ Composite. If you are pursuing an investment strategy of investing in large-cap, blue chip companies, then the most suitable benchmark would be the S&P 500.

The point to be made here is that if, over a period of time, the performance of your portfolio lags behind the performance of a suitable market benchmark, then you would improve your investment returns–and therefore increase your personal wealth–by investing in a mutual fund that mirrors that particular benchmark.

The Performance Chart

Whereas the Control Sheet and the Valuation Sheet can be updated at any time, the performance chart–along with the Valuation Sheet–should be updated at regular intervals, whether that be once a week or once a month. Those are the only times that any data will be entered in the Performance Chart.

The Valuation Sheet will provide performance information as of a specific date. It will not reveal performance data from the previous week or month. Therefore it would be very difficult for you to determine what the overall performance for either your benchmark or for your portfolio has been. Why is this important? A chart will provide you with a "picture" of your portfolio's performance over time. As the saying goes, "A picture is worth a thousand words." More important, the chart is empirical and can't be distorted by a reliance on your memory of past performance.

Creating a chart for the performance of your portfolio and your benchmark is a very simple procedure. The information that you will need has already been created. This procedure, however, requires the use of two charts—one containing the basic data and the other the chart created by the basic data. When you begin to construct your perform-ance charts, the charts themselves will be relatively meaningless since it takes a few weekly entries to generate a sufficient amount of perform-ance data to create a chart that will convey a sense of trends.

Generating the Data

In cell C3, entering the beginning value of your portfolio. Initially this will be the imaginary $250,000 that each of you is starting with. However, at the beginning of each new year, the amount entered in C3 will be the total portfolio value as of the end of the previous year. The percent increase or decrease in cell D3 will, of course, be 0.00% since you're just beginning. However, the next entry (C4) will almost cer-tainly be different from your original entry. To calculate the percentage increase or decrease in your portfolio's value, select cell D4. In the for-mula bar, enter the following formula: =(C4-C$3)/C$3.

The result of this computation will be the percentage increase or decrease in the performance of your portfolio, since the portfolio was started or since the beginning of the year.

Next, enter the closing value of the S&P 500 (or the NASDAQ Composite or whatever benchmark you opt for) in cell E3. Select cell F4. In the formula bar, enter the following formula: =(E4-E$3)/E$3.

The result of this computation will be the percentage increase or decrease in the performance of your chosen benchmark since the portfolio was started or since the beginning of the year.

All of your entries in this chart will be sequential, one row after the other. Therefore, all that's necessary to recreate the formula for the percentage increase in the portfolio value and in the benchmark value for each subsequent week is to highlight the cell containing the previous percentage change. Next, place your cursor in the lower right corner of that cell, wait for the cross to appear and drag to the cell below it. You won't have to do any "cutting" and "pasting" on this sheet.

To create the chart, highlight all of the dates and the two performance columns (B3 thru B40, then D3 through D40 and finally F3 thru F40). You should depress and hold the "Control" key while doing this. Be sure that you don't highlight the column headings–you only want the date and percentage changes. Click on the Excel Chart Wizard in the tool bar and follow the instructions to create your chart. Once the chart has been created, you can re-size it and drag it to a location close to the source data. If you want to print the chart, which I recommend, just click on the chart and black squares will appear in each corner. Select the print preview icon from the tool bar to be sure that you have, in fact, selected the chart. Then just hit the print icon.

You now have all of the tools that you will need to measure the performance of your portfolio. As the year progresses, you will have a very clear picture of how your portfolio is performing vis-à-vis your chosen benchmark.

By the way, these very same tools can–and should–be used for any of your existing investments.

			Entered (Bought)				Removed (Sold)			Net
A/1	B	C Company	D Date	E Shs.	F Price/Sh	G Cost	H Date	I Price/Sh	J Receipt	K Gain (Loss)
	1		04-Oct-99			8			-8	-16
	2									
	3									
	4									
	5									
	6									
	7									
	8									
	9									
	10									
	11									
	12									
	13									
	14									
	15									
	16									
	17									
	18									
	19									
	20									
	21									
	22									
	23									
	24									
	25									
	26									
	27									
	28									
	29									
	30									
	31									
	32									
	33									
	34									
	35									
	36									
	37									
	38									
	39									
	40									
			Totals			8			-8	-16
									249,984	

Control Sheet (above) Weekly Valuation Sheet (below)

A/1	B	C	D	E	F	G	H	I
2				Acquisition/Cost Data			Current Values	
3		Company	Symbol	Starting Date	Cost per Share	# of Shares	Per Share	Total
4	1							0
5	2							0
6	3							0
7	4							0
8	5							0
9	6							0
10	7							0
11	8							0
12	9							0
13	10							0
14	11							0
15	12							0
16	13							0
17	14							0
18	15							0
19							Total Market Value	0
20							Cash	0
21							Market Value + Cash	0

A / 1	B	C	D	E	F
2	Date	Portfolio	% Change	S&P 500	% Change
3	01-Jan	$250,000	0.0%	1282.81	0.0%
4	08-Jan				
5	15-Jan				
6	22-Jan				
7	29-Jan				
8	05-Feb				
9	12-Feb				
10	19-Feb				
11	26-Feb				
12	05-Mar				
13	12-Mar				
14	19-Mar				
15	26-Mar				
16	02-Apr				
17	09-Apr				
18	16-Apr				
19	23-Apr				
20	30-Apr				
21	07-May				
22	14-May				
23	21-May				
24	28-May				
25	04-Jun				
26	11-Jun				
27	18-Jun				
28	25-Jun				
29	02-Jul				
30	09-Jul				
31	16-Jul				
32	23-Jul				
33	30-Jul				
34	06-Aug				
34	13-Aug				
36	20-Aug				
37	27-Aug				
38	03-Sep				
39	10-Sep				
40	17-Sep				

Performance Data Sheet (top) Performance Chart (bottom)

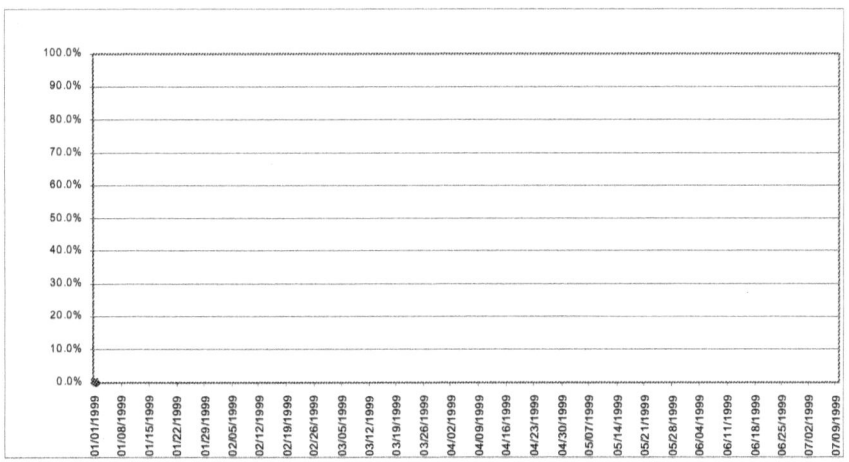

Chapter 6

Some Lessons Learned

"Scientists at leading research labs are starting to push the data-transmission capabilities of fiber-optic cable into the realm of the mind-boggling.

Setting a new record, researchers at Lucent's Bell Labs have for the first time managed to push an astonishing 3.28 terabits per second of data over a long stretch of fiber-optic cable.

A terabit—that's a trillion bits—is roughly equal to all the daily traffic on the Internet for the entire world. The Lucent fiber could transmit three times the daily global Internet traffic every second.

However, experts say the Bell Labs breakthrough is just the beginning.

In a matter of years, the fiber-optic cable being laid today by telecoms across the globe could be transmitting data at a rate of tens of thousands of terabits per second.

At these speeds, the entire written works of mankind could be beamed across the globe at the speed of light in just a few seconds."

Net Speed Ain't Seen Nothin' Yet, by Leander Kahney

http://www.wired.com/news/technology/0,1282,35079,00.html

After 3 Years, What Has Been Learned?

Psychiatrists say that learning from experience is enhanced if that experience is both visceral and intellectual. Whether dealing with real or fantasy money, the stock market can deliver both types of experiences. The breadth of knowledge that you acquire with your fantasy portfolio will be determined by the amount of time that you dedicate to making investment decisions.

Although I have added to my investment knowledge over the past three years, I have to admit that there are still facets of investing that perplex me. The indisputable number one issue that baffles me is knowing when to become defensive in anticipation of a market decline. How can you become defensive in anticipation of a market decline? The best and most conservative defensive strategy is simply to sell off portions of your portfolio. The by-product of being defensive is an increase in the amount of cash in your portfolio.

During the three-year exercise with my fantasy portfolio there were several occasions when the market averages trended down. However, in every one of those instances the downward trend didn't last very long and the market soon reversed to resume its upward trend. Not only did the upward trend resume, in each instance the market went on to new highs. Not one of those previous downtrends was as severe as the downtrend that occurred during the last two weeks of March 2000 and–in particular–the first two weeks of April 2000. The value of my portfolio went from a bit over $15 million to a bit over $7 million in less than a month. When a debacle of that magnitude occurs, it's important to analyze the market and economic conditions that existed prior to the decline. If specific causal conditions can be identified they can become important tools to avoid similar losses in the future.

On April 6, 2000, Mary Rowland of MSN Money Central wrote an enlightening article (*6 Signs for Spotting the Next Correction*) that identified six warning signs that existed prior to the sharp Nasdaq market decline. Here they are, along with my comments:

1. **The alarming rise in margin debt.** From September 1999 to February 2000 margin debt at brokerage firms increased 48% to a record $265.2 billion. What is remarkable about this increase is that as of March 10th the Nasdaq Composite Average had increased 24.1% since the beginning of the year. Most veteran investors know that market values must ultimately be related to revenue and earnings growth. It should have been obvious that the increase in the Nasdaq Composite during all of 1999 (+84.3%) and the first quarter of 2000 (+24.1%) was not sustainable for the balance of 2000. If ever market conditions were propitious for avoiding margin, this was certainly such a time.

    Buying stock on margin can produce inflated gains or expose investors to uncomfortable risks. When market values are increasing margin provides leverage. For example, an investor buying on margin can buy 200 shares of a particular stock for the same out-of-pocket expense as 100 shares. If the market value for that particular stock subsequently increases, rather than gaining $100 for every point increase in market value a margin investor would gain $200. In a bullish market environment, that can be very alluring.

    However, that allure is more than offset–in my opinion–with an extraordinary level of risk. Let me illustrate. Let's assume that an investor buys 200 shares of a $20 stock on margin. $2,000 of the $4,000 total cost is paid for by the investor and the other $2,000 is loaned to the investor by the brokerage firm. In Wall Street parlance, this investment would be financed by 50% equity (the investor's contribution) and 50% debt (the loan from the brokerage firm.)

No brokerage firm will *ever* allow declining market values to jeopardize the 50% loan that it extends to an investor buying on margin. To protect their loan, brokerage firms insist that an investor's equity–the current market value of the investment less the amount of the loan–must be equal to at least 25% of the current market value of the shares bought on margin. In a declining market it's the investor's equity that loses money, not the loan from the brokerage firm. The value of the loan remains constant. Therefore, if the market value of the stock in the previous illustration declines to $15 per share, the brokerage firm will issue a margin call to the investor. This whole business of margin calls represents a powerful market dynamic. For example, when the market dropped sharply in March-April, 2000, margin calls were one of the principle causes for the continuing decline. Every day that the market dropped, new margin calls were initiated. When customers wouldn't or couldn't provide the necessary increase in cash or securities, brokerages firms quickly sold the margined stock to protect the value of their loans. That selling inevitably caused the market to drop lower and the cycle became self-perpetuating. Savvy individual and institutional investors were well aware of these market dynamics. Although they were tempted to step in and buy stocks at market values that had become very appealing, they knew that those values were likely to drop even further. Consequently the normal buying that would have occurred was absent, as buyers waited for the margin liquidation to run its course.

Compounding the declining momentum was the fact that the decline occurred during tax-payment season. According to *The Wall Street Journal* ("Did Sales for Capital Gains Taxes Fuel Last Week's Massive Sell-Off?", April 18, 2000) individuals' capital gains taxes were expected to reach a record $99.7 billion for gains realized during 1999. Those taxes were payable by April 15, 2000. It seems likely that many of those individuals with capital gains taxes due raised the necessary cash by selling stock, thereby adding to the downward momentum created by brokers selling stocks to meet margin calls. The resulting market decline was not a pretty sight. The moral of the margin story is that if greed motivates you to buy stock on margin, be prepared for some unpleasantness when markets decline.

2. **The amazing expansion in multiples (price-to-earnings ratios) on the Nasdaq in February.** The problem that I have with this indicator is that stratospheric P/E ratios existed for at least a year prior to the March debacle. Consequently, if an investor had used this as a signal to get out of the market, he or she would not have participated in the extraordinary gains realized by the Nasdaq Composite during 1999 and early 2000.

    Nevertheless, as an incidental indicator, it certainly had value. Frequent articles, authored by scholars and market analysts, warned investors about the stratospheric market valuations, particularly for Internet stocks. The situation had become so extreme that some stocks were selling at price-to-sales valuations rather than the traditional and more conservative price-to-earnings valuations.

3.   The appearance of a new feature in Money magazine called
     "Millionaires to Be." As Ms. Rowland commented, "the pop-
     ular financial press is notorious for being a contrary indicator
     of market direction." Although Ms. Rowland demeans jour-
     nalists by explaining that they "often hop on a trend just as it
     is about to turn," my suspicion is that these folks do a very
     good job writing about the information that is fed to them by
     informed sources.

          I warned you that I was a bit of a cynic. However, if
          you were among the movers and shakers on Wall
          Street and your firms wanted to liquidate or reduce
          their inventory of stocks, wouldn't you want to
          inflate the investing public's expectations for higher
          market values? Is there a better method to
          accomplish that end than by feeding positive stories
          to the media to make sure that there would be lots of
          individual buyers at or near current market values
          for the stocks that you wanted to sell?

4.   The inverted yield curve. Perhaps I'm wrong, but I don't think
     that the average individual investor pays any attention to yield
     curves. Furthermore, interest rates had been increased five times
     during the previous six months and during that time the market
     was soaring to new highs, so this category might not have the
     relevance that it might have had in years gone by.

          Nevertheless, for those of you who don't compre-
          hend what an inverted yield curve is and who might
          want to include it in your arsenal of early warning
          signs, here's what it means. Normally long-term
          bond maturities have a higher yield than short-term
          maturities. The reason for this is that time represents
          an element of risk when investing in bonds.
          Therefore, the more distant the maturity, the higher

the risk and the higher the yield or interest rate that is demanded by bond investors. An inverted curve exists when interest rates for short-term maturities are higher than long-term maturities. The usual benchmarks for determining these rates are Treasury bills for the short-term maturities and the 25-year Treasury bond for the long-term maturities.

5. The news in February that many members of the Federal Reserve Open Market Committee wanted to raise the federal funds rate by 50 basis points rather than 25 basis points. A basis point represents 1/100 of one percentage point. In other words, an increase from 6.00% to 6.25% is an increase of 25 basis points.

> Once again I would hesitate to use this–on its own merits–as an early warning. After all, the same Committee had raised interest rates by 25 basis points four times prior to the February increase. I don't know if it was revealed after any of those prior increases that the Committee wanted to raise the rate by 50 basis points. Nevertheless, on several occasions prior to those increases it was widely anticipated that a 50 basis point increase might be forthcoming.

6. A switch in investor activity. Of the six indicators mentioned by Ms. Rowland, I think this is the best, as well as one that average individual investors can easily monitor. I can't improve on her explanation, so here are her words:

> "Investors had been buying on the dips. That shows investor optimism. One way to measure this is that the Nasdaq would generally close with the market on an upward momentum.

But in late February, investors began selling on rises. That indicates a shift to pessimism. The market would rally in the morning and then after lunch people would sell off and it would close with the momentum in a downward direction. The market was exhausted."

The March 21, 2000 issue of *Investor's Business Daily* contained an article by Christina Wise entitled "Top Investors Heed Market, Leading Stocks". Here are some useful indicators from that article:

"Like a romance gone sour, it's important to recognize the market's signs that the love affair is over."

Relative to the market...

"...a distribution day occurs when a major market average declines on heavier volume that the day before."

Relative to stocks...

"...reversed from the new high and closed in the bottom part of the day's range on expanded volume"

"If a stock gains ground on low volume, it may mean the market will not support the price increase over the long term."

"...volume shrinks significantly relative to what the trend had been in the advance–another sell signal."

"Trouble also may loom on the horizon if your winner sees its largest one-day drop since its advance began."

If you have the time, the talent and the temperament to monitor some or all of these indices, then you can probably avoid some of the inevitable market corrections that occur from time to time. However, most average individual investors will not have the required time, talent and temperament. For those of us who don't, here are some simpler guides to help with investment decisions.

Here's one method to simplify the process of deciding when to sell. Every time you decide to buy a stock, that decision ought to be based on research that you've done. Often times that research will consist of an article—or several articles—that you've read. Make a copy of that article and file it in an alphabetized notebook. If there were no articles that prompted your decision, then enter your reasons for buying in a notebook or investment diary, along with the date so that you can easily refer to those thoughts at any time in the future. Go through the same process of recording your thoughts when you make a decision to sell. This process of recording your reasons for buying and selling will force you to be more deliberate, which should result in better decisions.

The same process can be applied to your efforts to understand whether the economy is contracting, standing still or expanding. If you read an upbeat article about the economy that strengthens your resolve to be invested, make a copy of it. There will almost certainly be periods of time in the future when declines in the stock market will cause you to have questions about the economy and whether or not you should remain invested. Referring back to positive articles can provide you with the determination to remain invested and enable you to consider any dips in the market as being unavoidable and probably ephemeral.

Beware of Market Cycles.

Investment professionals know that the only way to make profitable investments is to buy low and sell high. When prices appear to be overvalued, the opportunity for profitable investing diminishes.

My work with quarterly earnings reports over the past couple of years has led me to believe that there is an almost predictable market cycle related to those earnings reports. You may recall that the majority of companies begin to report their earnings in mid-January, mid-April, mid-July, and mid-October. It's been my observation that markets often decline just prior to those time periods. This is particularly true in a bullish market environment when prices have advanced significantly in the three months prior to the earnings reporting season.

There always seems to be a logical and compelling explanation for these pre-earnings season market declines. During 1999 and 2000 the usual explanation was the rise in interest rates. Interestingly, however, the market almost always went higher as the earnings seasons progressed. The near-predictability of this sequence of events suggests that it's not a random phenomenon. The cynic in me suggests that when market values are deemed to be too high just prior to the earnings reporting seasons, Wall Street centers of influence suggest to the media that investors should be concerned about escalating interest rates, escalating energy costs or "irrational exuberance."

As investors read about and hear these negative stories, the natural urge is to preserve their profits by selling, which results in lower market valuations. Do you suspect, as I do, that the folks who fed these stories to the media are the ones who usually buy the stocks–at lower prices, of course–that have been sold by individual investors?

Cynicism aside, if you have assessed the state of the economy and of your selected industry and concluded that the economic expansion is still intact and that the forthcoming earnings reports will corroborate the continuing growth of revenues and earnings, it will be relatively easy for you to be insensitive to these cyclical market declines.

Defensive Strategies in Anticipation of Market Declines

A very good method to reflect either an aggressive or passive investment philosophy vis-à-vis the market is the amount of cash that you hold in your portfolio. When you're convinced that the economy is expanding and that this will be reflected in higher market values, your cash position should be kept at minimal levels. You want to have a high percentage of your money invested to take advantage of the rising market values.

On the other hand, when the economy appears to be headed for level or slow growth, the cash position of your portfolio should be increased. If you're correct in assessing that the market is headed for lower levels, the higher level of cash will provide you with a welcome source of available buying power to enable you to take advantage of the lower market prices. You can either add to the stocks already in your portfolio or replace some of the laggards with stocks that offer greater growth potential.

I'm not suggesting that you reduce the number of different stocks in your portfolio. Because of the uncertainties of the market I would recommend that you always maintain a level of fifteen stocks in your portfolio. If it appears that the market is getting overextended, reduce the number of shares that you have in some of your more profitable positions. Nobody is going to know precisely when the market will change direction, so by keeping the fifteen stocks in your portfolio you will still be participating in any further gains made in the market.

I didn't follow this advice in March of 2000. With the exception of roughly $1 million in cash I remained fully invested. The reason I remained fully invested is that I had confidence that the economy would continue to grow. More important, I was convinced that the information technology industry was just at the beginning of its growth curve. Had I read Ms. Rowland's article about the six signs to spot the next correction earlier in the year, I would clearly have become more defensive.

Some Additional Tools for Researching Individual Stocks

The market performance of individual stocks can be more volatile and more difficult to assess than the cycles of the economy or industry segments. One of the reasons for this volatility is that investors have a very wide variety of investment objectives. Those objectives can be as benign as simply wanting to move out of one stock into another stock that is perceived to offer greater potential. Also, not all investors have the same investment objectives. Some might be satisfied with a 25% gain in a particular stock, whereas others might be looking for a 100% or 200% gain from that same stock.

Investors have the opportunity to gain more information about individual stocks than they can about the economy or industry segments. However, interpreting that information can sometimes be confusing. For example, most average investors with an interest in high-tech companies would find it difficult to assess the unique competitive advantage that one company's product might have over another. This is one area where Wall Street analysts offer something of value.

However, there are other potential sources for that sort of interpretive information. For example, as mentioned earlier in this book, message boards represent significant potential. Most average investors will not be qualified to offer anything of value to message boards, particularly in regards to high technology. However, there are investors who do understand specific technological concepts and their input to message boards can be of great value. Their motivation to contribute–assuming that they are also investors in the company being discussed–is quite elementary. The market value of their investment will increase as more potential investors discover the unique competitive advantage offered by the company's products.

I visit message boards as a routine part of my research efforts. There are a couple of indicators on the message boards that influence my thoughts about the investment merits of a particular stock. First of all, I like to find a board where there have not been a lot of messages posted. For example, if a particular board on *Yahoo!* already has 25,000 messages posted, that suggests to me that I'm not very early in the discovery process. Second, if I notice that most of the messages deal with accusations and name-calling, that is almost an immediate turn-off. On the other hand, if there is a clear indication that intelligent discourse is the norm, that suggests to me that these folks are serious and that they fully comprehend the value of discovering and sharing useful investment information.

There is another potential source of interpretive information that can be made available on message boards. Mutual funds and investment management firms have traditionally shrouded their investment activity in secrecy. Usually investors can't learn about specific investments made by a mutual until 6 months later, or longer. In the case of investment management firms, it's almost impossible for the average investor to learn what stocks are in their portfolios. Why are they so secretive? One reason that I can think of is a fear that their mistakes would be visible to everyone. Another reason is that they suspect that other investors will try to emulate their investments. But think about that. Is potential emulation an undesirable consequence? I don't think so.

First of all, the average individual investor simply does not have enough wealth to emulate the diversified portfolio of most mutual funds or investment management firms. More to the point, those professional investors have the same overarching objective of every investor. They want to buy low and sell high. Using all of the databanks, talented analysts and rich sources of information available to them, they clearly have an advantage in the discovery process. In other words, they are more likely to be able to buy a stock at lower market values than the average individual investor.

Once their investment has been made in a specific company, wouldn't it be advantageous for them to inform the investing universe—individuals as well as institutions—of their discovery? The ensuing increase in buying activity, along with the growing reluctance to sell among existing shareowners, can only result in higher market values—precisely what they are striving to attain!

I know of at least one mutual fund that has literally opened its operations for the world to observe: the OpenFund (*http:www.openfund.com*).

Not only can investors learn about the stocks in the OpenFund portfolio on a daily basis, they can even observe the trades being made on its Internet home page. In fact, I have found this site to be one of the best sources of investment philosophy and market insights on the Internet–or anywhere else! If you don't have the time or temperament to follow the recommended procedures in this book, but want to participate in a well-managed mutual fund that invests in leading industries and leading companies, I would heartily recommend the OpenFund.

Some Words of Caution.

As enticing as having access to more and better investment information may seem, there does exist a potential negative. If all investors have access to and respond to widely available positive sources of information, the result can be a higher level of market volatility. Why? If the supply of a stock is decreased (existing shareholders not willing to sell) and the demand for that stock increases, the market value of that stock will go higher. And, the opposite is equally true when the widely accessible information is negative. With universal and instantaneous access to positive or negative investment information, the precipitous increase or decrease in the supply and demand for a specific stock will be condensed within a shorter period of time, resulting in sharply higher or sharply lower market values.

Fortunately, there is more to investing than just accessing information. That information has to be assimilated, interpreted and eventually acted upon. The processes of assimilation and interpretation will undoubtedly define and differentiate one investor's performance from another's in the future.

Keep in mind something that I learned many years ago: It is possible for individual investors to beat the market. However, it is *im*possible for *all* investors to beat the market, because the market is the sum of all investors. If you focus on the discovery concepts outlined in this book you will increase the likelihood that you will be one of those individual investors that beats the market.

A Few of My Successes...and Failures

Before analyzing some of my more notable successes and failures, it should be emphasized that this was a learning experience. Even though the performance of my fantasy portfolio over a three-year period–from April of 1997 to April of 2000–was outstanding, it could have been better.

You might reasonably ask how the performance could have been better. The answer is that I was continuously searching for new investment ideas. As new ideas were discovered, less appealing stocks had to be removed from the portfolio. I might add that during the entire three-year period I was working full-time. Hence I didn't have the necessary time to perform the in-depth research that would have enabled me to make better investment decisions.

Had that research been done, it is quite possible that my holding time for some stocks would have been longer, which would have resulted in significant gains in some instances. The following chart can illustrate this point:

Stock	Market Values		
	Average Buying Price	Average Selling Price	Subsequent High *
Ameritrade	27	27	264
Checkpoint Software	23	28	590
Citrix Systems	23	55	732
Conexant Systems	17	52	264
EFTC Corp	10	6	142
E-Tek Dynamics	20	34	315
Harmonic Lightwaves	16	10	314
I2 Technologies	21	27	446
Kopin	9	28	199
Leap Wireless	20	17	102
MRV Communications	14	14	199

* Adjusted for splits.

The message here is quite clear. If you don't do a good job of researching individual companies, there is a distinct risk that you will eliminate stocks from your portfolio that will subsequently soar in value. In reviewing all of the trades that occurred in my fantasy portfolio, there were only a few that declined in value after they were removed. You will always have some stocks that increase in value after you've removed them from your portfolio. Diligent research is the best way to lower the probability that this will impair the performance of your portfolio.

Just to review, here are some of the "quick" steps that I take in researching a particular company:

1. Carefully read some of the *Recent News* items, especially those that relate to recently released quarterly earnings reports.
2. Scan the company's *Profile.*
3. Review some of the recent postings in *Messages.*

4. Go to the company's *Home Page* to learn more about the company and its products.

Each of those items can be found in *Yahoo!* If you want dig deeper, research some of the documents filed by the company with the SEC at *www.freeedgar.com*. In fact, if time permits (and it should) I would recommend that no investment decision should be made unless and until you read one of the quarterly or annual reports filed by the company with the SEC.

There is one specific investment experience that I want to offer. Do you remember an earlier comment that sometimes your discovery can be too early? Here's a great illustration. I originally added *Superconductor Technology* (SCON) to my portfolio on January 3, 1988 at $3.50 per share. It was removed on July 28, 1988 at $5.00. Although I thought that their technology had significant potential and although I was aware that one of the premier Wall Street investment banking firms held a significant position in the stock, there weren't enough other investors who shared my views. The stock just didn't move. On September 16, 1988 I once again added SCON to the portfolio at $4.50 per share. It was removed on December 4, 1988 at a price of $4.00. My error with both of these trades was that I was trying to anticipate, rather than react to, the investment interest of others. You will note from the dates that I had not yet discovered the virtue of using the *extraordinary volume* or the *new highs* sources of information.

On February 9, 2000, SCON appeared on the *Bigchart* unusual activity list and once again it was added to my portfolio at a price of $12. Actually, had I been monitoring the daily new highs list on *Barcharts* I probably could have added SCON at half that price, or roughly $6 per share. SCON eventually became the single largest gainer in my fantasy portfolio. Before the end of February it shot up to a high of $115. I eliminated my entire position at prices ranging from $73 to $111. The total portfolio gain from this one-month holding period was more than $3 million!

In this illustration, I benefited from having researched SCON prior to the appearance of the stock on the unusual activity list. This resulted in my ability to make a very quick decision to add the stock to the portfolio. However, more important, it enabled me to be patient while the stock soared in value. Had I not been familiar with SCON's target market and the significant competitive advantage of its products, it would have been very tempting to take profits long before I actually did. Armed with that information I could wait until the market showed signs of topping out before removing the stock from my portfolio.

Whether you research a stock before or after its appearance on the new high or extraordinary volume lists, that research is very important. It's imperative that your reason for acquiring a stock be based on more than its appearance on one of these lists. This is particularly true in today's market environment. There are too many investors who shun the responsibility of doing their own research. These are the investors who jump into stocks that seem to have momentum and who quickly jump out when it appears that the momentum has dissipated.

There also appears to be a growing number of investors who have espoused the art of selling stocks short. They look for stocks that have displayed extraordinary increases in market value. Their philosophy seems to be that no stock should experience an unusual increase in market value within a short period of time. Ironically, some of the stocks that you will discover from the unusual activity and the new high lists are ideal candidates for these short-sellers. If you don't do your own independent research, you might find yourself trying to understand why the market value of your selected stock has begun to drop. If you visit one of the message boards, you'll probably discover that the short sellers are frequent posters. Most short-sellers are as guilty as a momentum investors in that they don't do the necessary research to determine the intrinsic value of a stock. Because they know that there is no limit to the amount of money they can lose if the market continues to move higher, they are very active and aggressive on message boards, disseminating strongly negative *opinions* about the stock that they have sold short (seldom do they use facts).

If, however, you have done the necessary research to feel comfortable about the longer-term prospects for your selected investment, you will not be bothered by the near-term machinations of other investors. You will recognize that, in today's market environment, near-term volatility is tantamount to a bump in the road. It's an extraordinarily comfortable feeling to know that the near-term zigs and zags of the market are irrelevant to your carefully researched judgment that the market value of your investment is ultimately going higher.

What's exciting about making this type of judgment is that the information currently available on the Internet empowers you to achieve the necessary level of comfort that you've made a good decision. There can be little doubt in anyone's mind that the quality and the usefulness of that information will almost certainly increase. But, you don't have to accept my word. The following appeared in the August 23, 1999 issue of *Barron's Online.*

Predictions:

1. *By 2005, most people will get their financial information online.*
2. *By 2005, the "pipeline" problem will be solved.*
3. *True interactivity will enable investors to use tools and data seamlessly.*
4. *"Middlemen" will be squeezed out as costs drop.*
5. *Data will be a commodity, but people will pay a premium for reliable information and analysis.*
6. *Traditional information and service providers will adapt or die.*
7. *Moore's Law will continue to drive the market: smarter, better, faster.*
8. *Investors will be more empowered than ever.*

Appendix

The Long Boom: A History of the Future, 1980-2020 (excerpts)

http://www.hotwired.com/wired/5.07//longboom.html
We're facing 25 years of prosperity, freedom, and a better environment for the whole world. You got a problem with that?

By Peter Schwartz and Peter Leyden

A bad meme–a contagious idea–began spreading through the United States in the 1980s: America is in decline, the world is going to hell, and our children's lives will be worse than our own. The particulars are now familiar: Good jobs are disappearing, working people are falling into poverty, the underclass is swelling, crime is out of control. The post-Cold War world is fragmenting, and conflicts are erupting all over the planet. The environment is imploding–with global warming and ozone depletion, we'll all either die of cancer or live in Waterworld. As for our kids, the collapsing educational system is producing either gun-toting gangsters or burger-flipping dopes who can't read.

By the late 1990s, another meme began to gain ground. Borne of the surging stock market and an economy that won't die down, this one is more positive: America is finally getting its economic act together, the world is not such a dangerous place after all, and our kids just might lead tolerable lives. Yet the good times will come only to a privileged few, no more than a fortunate fifth of our society. The vast majority in the United States and the world face a dire future of increasingly desperate poverty. And the environment? It's a lost cause.

But there's a new, very different meme, a radically optimistic meme: We are watching the beginnings of a global economic boom on a scale never experienced before. We have entered a period of sustained growth that could eventually double the world's economy every dozen years and bring increasing prosperity for–quite literally–billions of people on the planet. We are riding the early waves of a 25-year run of a greatly expanding economy that will do much to solve seemingly intractable problems like poverty and to ease tensions throughout the world. And we'll do it without blowing the lid off the environment.

If this holds true, historians will look back on our era as an extraordinary moment. They will chronicle the 40-year period from 1980 to 2020 as the key years of a remarkable transformation. In the developed countries of the West, new technology will lead to big productivity increases that will cause high economic growth–actually, waves of technology will continue to roll out through the early part of the 21st century.

Sitting here in the late 1990s, it's possible to see how all the pieces could fall into place. It's possible to construct a scenario that could bring us to a truly better world by 2020. It's not a prediction, but a scenario, one that's both positive and plausible. Why plausible? The basic science is now in place for five great waves of technology–personal computers, telecommunications, biotechnology, nanotechnology, and alternative energy–that could rapidly grow the economy without destroying the environment. This scenario doesn't rely on a scientific breakthrough, such as cold fusion, to feed our energy needs. Also, enough unassailable trends–call them predetermined factors–are in motion to plausibly predict their outcome.

One hundred years ago, the world went through a similar process of technical innovation and unprecedented economic integration that led to a global boom. New transportation and communications technologies–railroads, telegraphs, and telephones–spread all over the planet, enabling a coordination of economic activity at a level never seen before.

Today, the United States has a similarly crucial leadership role to play. There are purely practical reasons for this. The United States has the single largest economy in the world, a market with a big influence on the flow of world trade. It has the biggest research and scientific establishment by far. Since the demise of the Soviet Union, no other country features a comparable array of university research facilities, corporate industrial labs, and nonprofit think tanks. That combination of a huge economy and a scientific elite gives the United States the world's strongest military: the country can develop the weapons and pay the bills. For the next 15 years at the very least, America will be the preeminent military power. These reasons alone ensure that the United States, regardless of the intentions of its leaders, will have a huge influence on any future scenario. But the role of the United States is more involved, more complicated than that.

The United States is the great innovator nation, the incubator of new ideas. Just as the new technologies of the early Industrial Revolution were born in England, the vast majority of innovations in the computer and telecommunications fields are happening now in the United States. Americans are fundamentally shaping the core technologies and infrastructure that will be at the foundation of the 21st century.

The vast array of problems to solve and the sheer magnitude of the changes that need to take place are enough to make any global organization give up, any nation back down, any reasonable person curl up in a ball. That's where Americans have one final contribution to make: optimism, that maddening can-do attitude that often drives foreigners insane. Americans don't understand limits. They have boundless confidence in their ability to solve problems. And they have an amazing capacity to think they really can change the world.

Introduction: Into the Wild Frontier

http://www.businessweek.com/1997/25/b35321.htm
Back in 1979, if you had visited Xerox's Palo Alto Research Center, you would have literally seen the future of computing. The precursor

of Windows. The computer mouse. The laser printer. And a local-area network, newly dubbed Ethernet. If you had then broadened the tour, scientists at AT&T Bell Labs and IBM could have give you a spiffy prediction about digital phone switches and computer memory, anticipating developments that arrived just this year.

Ah, but you didn't make those visits, and now the opportunity of a lifetime has passed. Or has it? The world has changed a lot since then. Computer skills are much more diffuse. Exotic new technologies abound. But one thing remains true: In a handful of the world's outstanding computer labs, the shape of tomorrow is as plain to see as it was 20 years ago. What those labs are doing now will set the agenda for computing over the next 15 to 20 years.

Why do we know all this is coming? Two reasons. First, because we can bank on the same forces that unleashed the PC revolution 25 years ago: shrinking silicon circuits and faster communications infrastructure. The pace of change is actually accelerating now, says Richard Howard, director of wireless research at Lucent Bell Laboratories. In the next two decades, we'll see explosive growth of communications, computing, memory, wireless, and broadband technology.

The other reason we can divine future trends is that the seeds are already widely sown—both in the market and in dozens of computer research labs. Invisible computers? Chipmakers ship about 3.5 billion of those every year in the form of embedded or "real-time" processors. That's nearly 50 times the number of microprocessors sold in boxes with keyboards and monitors. An economy-class car has a dozen hidden microprocessors controlling the engine, brakes, and other systems. A Mercedes has about 60. Reconfiguring machines? That's what field-programmable gate arrays are. They're on the market now—though engineers have barely begun to tap their power.

Even computers that become part of our bodies are not so far-fetched. According to Peter Cochrane, head of research at British Telecommunications PLC, surgeons have performed about 17,000 cochlear implants on patients with hearing loss. "These people are already walking around with chips in their heads," he says.

All of this is on the street right now. But it pales beside what's in the labs.

Scientist envisages a home life served by mass of wee computers
http:www.phillynews.com/inquirer/98/Jan/22/tech.life/CHIP22.htm

Palo Alto, Calif.–Sitting in his cluttered corner office at Xerox's Palo Alto Research Center, Mark Weiser is describing a future in which computers embedded into everyday objects–your wallet, your kitchen appliances, your chair, your car–communicate with one another as you go about your daily routine.

For one thing, you won't have to wonder whether you need to buy milk while standing clueless in the grocery store aisle.

"If your refrigerator watches you take the milk carton in and out every day and your refrigerator could talk to your wallet," Weiser said, "then when you went to the store, the wallet could tell the milk cartons that you need milk. And the milk cartons can then say to you, 'Hey, buy me. You're out of milk.'"

Weiser, PARC's chief technologist, is credited in research circles with coming up with the concept now known as ubiquitous computing, what some see as then next revolution in computer science.

The first part of the ubiquitous computing equation has already fallen into place as microprocessors have infiltrated everyday devices in middle-class homes–from the TV remote control to the digital alarm clock. The advent of the Internet and wireless technologies already can allow some of these devices to communicate with one another. But Weiser is looking seven to 10 years ahead, when even the middle class–not just Microsoft mogul Bill Gates–may be living in high-tech houses.

No one is certain quite how the scenarios will unfold. Will there be clocks that can find out the correct time after a power failure? What about a microwave oven capable of downloading new recipes from the

Internet? How about children's toys that can be recycled through the installation of new software?

If Weiser is right, we could soon be entering the third revolution in computing. The first revolution, he said, was the development of the mainframe computer, one large box shared by many people. The second wave was the development of the PC, in which one person used one computer. The third era, ubiquitous computing, is actually somewhat of the opposite of the mainframe era: Instead of one computer sharing many people, you have one person sharing many computers.

While Weiser is hardly the most high-profile thinker in Silicon Valley–he has been more of a behind-the-scenes guy–his combination of hard-core computer science and sportiveness has helped him in developing concepts that one day may affect the lives of all Americans.

That's how Weiser comes up with his seemingly incredible ideas. Take shopping. Many presume that the Internet and electronic commerce will mark the end of physical shopping. But not Weiser. "People like to shop. They just need some help. They like to do the fun things, exploring stores, trying things on, looking for bargains," Weiser said, leaning back in a chair amid his office clutter. "But maybe a week later, they go back to the store, trying to find that special shirt that really looked good on them to see if it was marked down. And they can't remember where it is again."

Enter computers everywhere. "If the shirt had a computer on it that was talking to the network, it could communicate its Internet address to the computer in your pocket by the time you enter the store" and even disclose whether the price has gone down, Weiser said. "Imagine that. Shopping would be even more fun and easier."

New Math: One Plus One Equals Four
http://www.FORBES.com/assap/1202961/html/RICH_WILLIS.htm

In the information age, conventional mathematics is obsolete. Economics and accounting, which are based on an outdated version of mathematics, are likewise obsolete. They key is to recognize that information arithmetic is fundamentally different from object arithmetic. In the information age, one plus one equals four.

Imagine a meeting where all attendees bring one tangible object and one idea. The objects and ideas are shared. Everyone leaves with only one object, but each departs with as many ideas as there are attendees. What results from the meeting is distinctly different from what was brought to the meeting. Whenever ideas are shared, the result is always greater than the sum of the parts.

This fundamental law of information, in which one can give something yet retain it, is the most vitally important concept to grasp if one is to understand the information age. Our language frequently impedes our comprehension of this idea. When we use words such as give, transfer, deliver, receive, steal, etc., we assume that the transferred item no longer resides with its originator. With information, ownership of ideas, facts, and knowledge is not exclusive. It does not leave the originator.

Rules and laws derived from the world of physical objects are frequently applied to the world of information and ideas, with adverse results. When more than half the software in use throughout the world is estimated to be illegally copied, something is seriously wrong with our system of using and protecting intellectual property. Surely the needs of content creators, publishers, and users can be better balanced without making criminals of millions of people. But to conceive of a better system, we must first contemplate the new questions that arise when many people "own" the same information.

The world of information is infinite. Unlike capital, labor, the money supply, or physical resources, there are virtually no limits to the knowledge and understanding that can spread throughout the world. This limitlessness applies whether it is raw data of questionable utility, information that imparts something genuinely relevant, or knowledge that conveys meaning and insight. Pessimists, such as Jeremy Rifkin, who worry about the "information haves" exploiting the "information have-nots," erroneously apply physical object-based concerns to the intangible world of information. Physical objects are expensive to duplicate for everyone who might want them. Information and knowledge have no such limits. They can be used by everyone, simultaneously.

The allocation of scarce resources by markets and governments has fueled many a political and economic debate. In the information age this key commodity, information, is anything but scarce. Since no one has to lose anything when someone else gains knowledge, our economic models of allocation need a fundamental overhaul. We have entered an age in which the possibilities should be as boundless as the flows of information around us. Yet far too many of us are worrying about how the pie is being carved up, rather than enjoying the feast of a rapidly expanding pie.

Economy Counts Gains Behind Digital Advances

Russ Britt, Investor's Business Daily

http://www.investors.com/stories/IF/1999/Jan/19/120.html
It's unanimous.

From Federal Reserve Chairman Alan Green span to economists, from corporate chieftains to Department of Commerce bureaucrats, there is a consensus: Nothing has fueled the longest peacetime economic expansion in the U.S. quite like technology.

"This is the second industrial revolution," said John Chambers, chief executive of Cisco Systems Inc., the largest seller of networking gear.

That's not just a profit-minded executive talking. Federal officials agree. In fact, Greenspan concurred with Chambers' assessment during a speech in July.

"The United States is currently confronting what can best be described as another industrial revolution," Greenspan said at the time. "The rapid acceleration of computer and telecommunications technologies is a major reason for the appreciable increase in our productivity in this expansion, and is likely to continue to be a significant force in expanding standards of living into the 21st century."

And in its report last year on "The Emerging Digital Economy," even the Commerce Department draws Industrial Revolution comparisons.

Unlike that era, though, the Internet took only a few years to gain widespread influence. It took decades for such tools of the Industrial Revolution as electricity and steam engines to proliferate, the report notes.

"More than 100 million people around the world, most of whom had never heard of the Internet four years ago, now use it to do research, send (electronic) mail to friends, make requests for bids from suppliers and shop for cars or books," the report said. "The Internet's pace of adoption eclipses all other technologies that preceded it."

Tech's influence started making its mark when computers became more sophisticated in the early '90s. A quick burst in PC sales around '93 and '94 helped the nation recover from the '90-'91 recession.

Then the nation quickly discovered the Internet. That put technology's role on a much grander scale as communication extended globally. Some say the Internet's potential is only scratching the surface.

"In short, it will change every industry," said Cisco's Chambers. "It creates a level playing field between companies, regardless of size."

Chambers projects that by '03, 80% to 90% of all new jobs will be technology-oriented. He says the potential for electronic commerce could reach into the trillions of dollars in revenue in the next decade.

It also appears that technology's effect on gross domestic product is growing at a rapid clip. In April, the Commerce Department said technology accounts for at least 8.2% of the nations's GDP, up from 6.4% in '93.

Although unwilling to dub technology as the economy's one-magic elixir, Commerce Undersecretary Shapiro says its influence stretches far beyond conventional GDP numbers. He points out technology accounts for 15% of GDP growth.

There also have been huge gains in the stock market. Since March '91, when the last recession ended, an index of 10 technology stocks tracked by Investor's Business Daily has shot up 856%. In that same span, the S&P 500 rose 230%.

Technology has changed the landscape by which businesses operate, says Gordon Eubanks, chief executive of software maker Symantec Corp.

Advances in software and networking let companies compete in areas they never dreamed possible before, Eubanks says. He says that this is having a secondary, yet more powerful, impact on the economy than the initial effect on jobs and revenue.

"The secondary impact is things like bringing more spending power to the economy—the fact that more industries are more competitive because of it," Eubanks said. *"It allows people to be more competitive. It's hard to imagine how people ran these companies before we had these (advances)."*

www.ingramcontent.com/pod-product-compliance
Lightning Source LLC
Chambersburg PA
CBHW030741180526
45163CB00003B/882